"At some point in every Christian's life, God intervenes to show us that what we thought to be our home isn't—and sometimes, only a lifetime later does one see that this was actually good news. Mike Cosper is one of the sharpest thinkers in the Christian world, and also one of the most creative. This book includes cultural analysis, personal lament, and biblical reflection. If you've ever felt the pain of losing home—and if you want to learn how to long for something better—this is the book for you."

Russell Moore, editor in chief of *Christianity Today*

"*Land of My Sojourn* is a beautifully told story of a life of grace, grief, and gratitude, an immensely personal, memoir-like narrative that seamlessly weaves together Mike Cosper's predictably wise musings on Scripture, culture, politics, power, trauma, the church, and more. It's a story so well told, truthfully told, and generously told that you'll likely find some of your own story in it too. What a gift!"

Chuck DeGroat, professor of pastoral care at Western Theological Seminary and author of *When Narcissism Comes to Church*

"There are a lot of Christians—like Mike Cosper and like me—who have experienced a lot of grace in church, and who have also been deeply wounded in that same place. Through telling his own story, Cosper grapples deeply with the religious PTSD that is all too familiar to so many, and he describes how he has come through brokenness and despair. He's not in a rush to fully heal. He's still invested in a local church, but with a moderated emotional attachment. I think many Christians put too much hope in the idea of church and in their religious leaders. Cosper's book shows why that's a mistake, and it traces a path toward a more balanced approach."

Jon Ward, author of *Testimony* and *Camelot's End*

"In this riveting account of the rise and fall of a church full of artists in Louisville, Kentucky, Mike Cosper, as their sojourner founding pastor, chronicles the longings of 'the particular lives of particular people' to reveal the deep rifts of culture-wars dysfunction in the evangelical communities of our times. Mike's honest introspection through this revelatory writing is a healing balm for our own journeys of exile, to remind us that even in such painful experiences of brokenness of faith communities there is yet grace present. Like Elijah under a broom tree, we are led out of our utter despair and debilitation into a place of sustenance and hope, to look up and see that we are not alone."

Makoto Fujimura, artist and author of *Art+Faith: A Theology of Making*

land
of my
sojourn

x————————x

the landscape
of a faith lost
and found

mike cosper

An imprint of InterVarsity Press
Downers Grove, Illinois

InterVarsity Press
P.O. Box 1400 | Downers Grove, IL 60515-1426
ivpress.com | email@ivpress.com

InterVarsity Press® is the publishing division of InterVarsity Christian Fellowship/USA®. For more information, visit intervarsity.org.

All Scripture quotations, unless otherwise indicated, are taken from The Holy Bible, New International Version®, NIV®. Copyright © 1973, 1978, 1984, 2011 by Biblica, Inc.™ Used by permission of Zondervan. All rights reserved worldwide. www.zondervan.com. The "NIV" and "New International Version" are trademarks registered in the United States Patent and Trademark Office by Biblica, Inc.™

Scripture quotations marked MSG are taken from The Message, copyright © 1993, 2002, 2018 by Eugene H. Peterson. Used by permission of NavPress. All rights reserved. Represented by Tyndale House Publishers.

While any stories in this book are true, some names and identifying information may have been changed to protect the privacy of individuals.

Published in association of the literary agent Don Gates of The Gates Group, www.the-gates-group.com.

Lyrics from Bill Mallonee, "Resplendent," used with permission.

The publisher cannot verify the accuracy or functionality of website URLs used in this book beyond the date of publication.

Cover design: David Fassett
Interior design: Jeanna Wiggins
Cover image: © Ed Freeman / Getty Images

ISBN 978-0-8308-4734-1 (print) | ISBN 978-0-8308-4735-8 (digital)

Printed in the United States of America ∞

Library of Congress Cataloging-in-Publication Data
Names: Cosper, Mike, 1980- author.
Title: Land of my sojourn : the landscape of a faith lost and found / Mike
   Cosper.
Description: Downers Grove, IL : IVP, [2024]
Identifiers: LCCN 2023037477 (print) | LCCN 2023037478 (ebook) | ISBN
   9780830847341 (print) | ISBN 9780830847358 (digital)
Subjects: LCSH: Leadership–Religious aspects–Christianity. | Church.
Classification: LCC BV4597.53.L43 C68 2024 (print) | LCC BV4597.53.L43
   (ebook) | DDC 253–dc23/eng/20231026
LC record available at https://lccn.loc.gov/2023037477
LC ebook record available at https://lccn.loc.gov/2023037478

30 29 28 27 26 25 24 | 13 12 11 10 9 8 7 6 5 4 3 2 1

X————————————————————————

For "all who have sailed on rivers of heartache,"

my fellow travelers and sojourners,

the prone to wander and those that kept the light in the window.

And most of all for Sarah, Dorothy, and Maggie.

Just a few more miles to go . . .

————————————————————————X

Contents

Introduction

When Gravity Fails

"I'm not sure we can stick with you on this," Greg said.

We were sitting in a large executive suite on the upper levels of an old, turn-of-the-century building. A wide antique window behind him framed the setting sun, which cut a low band of gold across an otherwise iron-gray sky. I didn't know Greg well. We'd been introduced earlier that year when I began putting together plans for a new media-focused nonprofit to serve Christians in the marketplace. I'd pitched him the idea and asked him to consider being involved in a couple of ways as we launched. He'd taken it a step further, expressing interest in helping to build certain elements of the ministry with me.

By the time of this meeting we had planned not only to work together on the nonprofit but also to collaborate on equipping resources for Christian leaders inside several companies. Suddenly, he hit the brakes.

"Help me understand," I said.

He leaned forward, resting his elbows on his knees, wringing his hands, and looking at the floor. "I just think you've got this election thing wrong," he said.

"What do you mean," I asked. "The Trump thing?" There was a long silence.

Only a few days earlier the now-infamous *Access Hollywood* tape had leaked, in which then-presidential candidate Donald Trump described how fame allowed him to get away with anything, including grabbing women "by the p____." In a newsletter I'd written what I thought was a fairly common-sense analysis from a Christian perspective—that he had failed every character test by which other presidents and politicians had been measured. No one put it better than Albert Mohler, at least at the time, when he said that were he to endorse Donald Trump, consistency would demand that he write a letter of apology to Bill Clinton as well for vocally opposing the former president's sexual misconduct. (Notably, Mohler did endorse Trump in 2020. As of this writing, no such "consistent" apology has come.)

My point in writing the newsletter wasn't (as William F. Buckley once famously phrased it) to stand athwart history yelling "Stop!" I didn't presume to stand in front of a steam train on principle. Rather, I thought I was reiterating common-sense ideas in an election cycle in which wild voices from the fringe were being amplified in new and horrible ways. Honestly, I thought I was in the majority on Trump's character. I was, however, *not* in the majority.

"Look," I said, "I understand that for some folks this is a binary decision. I happen to disagree, but I understand."

"That's not it," Greg said. "It's more . . . important than that."

Weird emphasis. "I just think it's time for us all to get behind him—Trump. Because, well . . ."

Now Greg sat up. He looked me right in the eye. "Finally, someone is going to stand up for the White man."

To that point in my life I'd been a pastor working at the intersection of faith and culture. Leading a ministry for artists and church musicians, writing about movies, music, and TV, and teaching about politics, public witness, and faithfulness in the marketplace. No doubt, there were places I parted ways with the Christian conservatives in the generations before me, but these were mostly differences in degree, not in principle, that left plenty of common ground to collaborate on. This meeting, this break, read as something else. Something tectonic. It hit like a thunderclap.

The 2016 election cycle had been weird. The gloves had come off when the Republicans were still debating each other. Mockery and derision set the tone. Trump seemed to only gain momentum the more crass he became. And some pockets of the internet were combining their support of the man with other, unsettling sentiments. But that was the internet. The internet couldn't be real. Now it was across the table. Someone who was a collaborator ten minutes ago now was a stranger to me. It was disorienting.

In the aftermath I began to wonder if this could be the norm. Had the animating concerns that fell under the banners of "conservatism," "traditional values," "religious liberty," or even "evangelicalism" been a veneer, a lure to co-opt people in the church into the service of ugly, identitarian politics? To put it a little differently, what had I been giving my life to for the past fifteen years?

I remember seeing *Space Camp* in the theaters in 1986. It's an 80's classic starring Kate Capshaw, Lea Thompson, Tom Skerritt, and Joaquin Phoenix. In it a ragtag group of misfits are grouped for a week of space camp. Due to Promethean mistakes and good old-fashioned hijinks, their team is accidentally launched into space aboard an underequipped space shuttle. High adventure ensues. Lots of learning. Lots of hugging.

One scene has stuck with me for almost forty years. Andie, the kids' camp counselor, heads out on a spacewalk to collect oxygen tanks to resupply the shuttle. When she can't quite reach them, Max—the youngest and smallest of the group—is sent out to help. While tugging on a tank, Max loses his grip and goes hurtling into space, untethered to anything at all. That image—tumbling into the vacuum of space, no gravity to bring you back, just an eternal drift into blackness—scared the bejeezus out of six-year-old me. It still does.

Finally, someone is going to stand up for the White man.

With these words a switch flipped. Gravity vanished. I could only watch, stunned, as the ground drifted away beneath me. The year

2016 felt like that 1980s nightmare came to life. It was, for lack of a better word, an apocalypse. A revealing. I found myself in a dark landscape without a tether. Friendships, partnerships, my sense of place in my church and city, the broader evangelical community—none of it held together anymore. This meeting was the beginning of the season that would leave me feeling completely adrift.

In Ernest Hemingway's *The Sun Also Rises*, someone asks Mike—a hard-drinking and self-pitying Scottish war veteran—how he went broke. "'Two ways,' Mike said. 'Gradually, then suddenly.'"

I've discovered that spiritual disillusionment happens that way too. You crash into this sense that faith as you knew it doesn't make sense anymore, but when you look backward, you see signs and evidence you didn't take seriously at the time.

Looking back, the first glint of disillusionment I see happened in 2012, not long after the murder of Trayvon Martin. I preached a sermon from Ephesians 2, where Paul describes how Jesus breaks down the walls of hostility that separate men and women of different races. I took that sermon as an opportunity to speak to the broader racial tensions that were emerging in our country but also as an opportunity to help our church see the unifying beauty of Christ as we moved into a more diverse neighborhood and began to pursue a more multicultural approach to ministry. Similar to the newsletter in 2016, I didn't think I was saying anything controversial. Rather, I thought I was helping the church find language for taking the next steps with these issues.

In the sermon I took no political stances. I simply preached about compassion and empathy for our Black brothers and sisters, especially those in the neighborhood around our church. I tried to relay their stories—as they had told them to me—of how everyday experiences for Black Americans differed from our majority-White congregation's. I talked about how fear of being called a racist made many White Christians hypersensitive to discussions of race and invited the community to make space for listening to the experiences and perceptions of Black and Latino members of our church. Maybe, I suggested, some of our assumptions are wrong—especially when they've been formed without any input from minority voices. Maybe there was some room for repentance.

This was years before critical race theory would become a political boogeyman, before Black Lives Matter would become a controversial organization, before *woke* would be co-opted by the political right and used as a pejorative. Nonetheless, saying that Black and White Americans had very different everyday experiences, suggesting that racism was still an issue in America, and reading a few short quotes from Martin Luther King Jr. and Frederick Douglass (along with lots of Scripture) created no small amount of controversy. After preaching, I was harangued in the parking lot and the church received angry calls and emails for several weeks. Some members called for an apology or my removal from the staff.

At the time I didn't have categories for understanding those reactions. Later, when I wrote several blog posts about race, police shootings, and how White Christians could join their neighbors in compassion and lament, the response grew even more threatening and vitriolic.

In 2012 I tried to be open. I reminded myself that defensive reactions could easily be rooted in fear and shame. An anxious response to the accusation of racism might not be racism itself. Post-2016 all of this started to read differently for me. I still believe anxiety and fear can play a role but only as part of a larger story about deceived and corrupted moral imaginations.

Finally, someone is going to stand up for the White man.

Those were far from the last comments I'd hear about Trump as a defender of White America. Along with increased overt racism, older and subtler ideas I'd heard from White Christians reemerged. Insinuations I'd heard for years about the poor theology of the Black church or the pagan roots of rap, hip-hop, R&B, and even the blues, about the origins of poverty or fatherlessness in Black communities—all of them emerged in a new, uglier light.

In the days and weeks after my meeting with Greg, other donors backed out of their commitments or lost interest in my nonprofit. I found myself without sufficient resources and the dream failed to launch. So began a long vocational journey that would stretch several years and pass through a landscape where Christian leaders I'd respected for decades continued to realign with the new political reality, writing op-eds about how border walls were biblical, how every election was binary, and how we had to have patience for a baby Christian like Donald Trump. Who were we to judge the fanatical online followers or their anti-semitic memes? Weren't the Clintons worse? Those who refused to support Trump lost jobs, lost speaking opportunities, and began long seasons in the desert.

The world at large became seemingly alien, but the disruptions didn't stop with politics and race. Another apocalypse opened up in 2016. Very close to home. Tensions that had nothing to do with political rhetoric or race came to a head in my church, the church I helped plant and had pastored for fifteen years. Concerns about the leadership at our church emerged, met with doubts that the concerns were valid. People took sides. Relationships stretched thin. I happened to share the concerns about a lack of organizational health that had grown impossible to ignore. My wife, Sarah, and I found ourselves cut off from friendships that were decades old. Our wounds, long masked by the momentum of ministry, began to surface, and the physical and psychological toll of spending years in a toxic culture caught up with me. I crashed. Physically and spiritually exhausted, isolated and brokenhearted, I saw a community I loved—one I had poured my heart and soul into—on the verge of breaking apart.

Around that time my friend Mike Frazier invited me and my family to a retreat house his church owned just outside Savannah, Georgia. I owed my publisher revisions and edits for the manuscript for *Recapturing the Wonder*, and my family needed the time away to decompress from all that had taken place, so a retreat sounded inviting.

In Savannah our kids played in the shade of a live oak tree in front of the house, turning the moss, sticks, and twigs into fairy houses. We would all watch in laughter as one neighbor would turn off the main road near the house and slow to a crawl and let his shaggy brown dog leap from the passenger door to chase the car at breakneck speed the rest of the way down the dirt road. And Sarah and I would sit in silence on the front porch of the little house. Drinking coffee and watching the kids, yes. And her with a book and me with a pile of papers that I would occasionally leaf through and mark up with a red pen. But really, we were shell-shocked, with hardly a word to say to one another.

Rereading *Recapturing the Wonder* felt surreal. I'd written most of the manuscript before leaving my job at the church and before the upheavals of 2016—before the apocalypse, the shattered community, the disorientation that had affected the weariness that we were now shouldering. That book is about the way modernity and secularism have reshaped our imaginations. How their relentless assertion that the only meaning in the world is what we can touch and measure contests all our spiritual experiences and leaves us cynical and disenchanted. Quarantined from spiritual reality. It suggests a variety of ways of resisting such a flattening of the world, rebuilding our spiritual imaginations through historic Christian practices like prayer, meditative Bible study, and fasting.

I still believe what I wrote in that book, and I still believe that there's an urgent need for Christians to address the way our world hollows the experience of transcendence. But what had begun to open to me was another way that faith could be contested: from within. If the danger of modernity's pressures on the Christian faith resulted in disenchantment, the new danger I was confronting was leading to disillusionment.

We spent our last night in Savannah with Frazier and his wife, Cheryl. We sat up late, Sarah and Cheryl talking in the kitchen and dishing out mountains of ice cream and marshmallows for our kids. Frazier and I sat in another room. As I processed the preceding months, he read the weariness on my face and in my posture. He asked question after question, surfacing sadness, weariness, and physical exhaustion that I didn't even know were there.

Before leaving he asked about spiritual disciplines—what did prayer look like for me, how was I approaching the Scriptures? I confessed that Scripture was difficult for me. I'd seen it used so often lately as a bludgeon. I struggled to hear it now. Mostly, when I opened a Bible, it was to the Psalms.

"I want to suggest something for you," he said and picked up a Bible off a side table. He turned to 1 Kings 18 and read the story of Elijah confronting the prophets of Baal. He continued to chapter 19, to Elijah lying under the broom tree in the desert, pleading for God to take his life.

When he was finished, he closed the Bible and set it back on the table. He explained nothing to me; he just sat silent there for a long, awkward moment. "You know," he said, "I wonder what might happen if you just spent some time with that story. Especially chapter 19—with tired Elijah."

I nodded. We got up to leave shortly after, and I walked out into a pitch-black Savannah night, back into zero gravity.

Not long after that trip to Savannah, I visited the Holy Land with a group of friends. That trip deepened the grip that landscape held on my imagination. The golden light of the Old City at night, the lush green of the Jezreel Valley, the gnarled bark of olive trees in the Garden of Gethsemane. After I returned home and continued to navigate the turbulence of my faith, those images kept returning to my mind. They haunted me even as my faith grew thin and brittle.

So, when I finally took Frazier's advice about Elijah, the desert the prophet crashed in was tangible to me in ways that kindled my spiritual imagination. I had been where Elijah had been.

In time Elijah led me to Mount Tabor, the mountain of the transfiguration, where the old prophet stood and talked with Jesus and Moses while Peter, James, and John watched in awe. This story was far from new to me, so it wasn't a surprise to find those men there. It was a surprise to find someone else there: me.

Reading that story I found myself echoing Peter's words and emotions, that brilliant moment making sense to me in ways I couldn't have imagined before. I then followed Peter onward—to Jerusalem, Gethsemane, and another mountain: Golgotha. And eventually back to the place his story began, on the shores of the Sea of Galilee. As I saw those echoes of my story, I discovered that the journey of my own inner life was nothing new, just as Peter's was nothing new. His own life had echoed the ups and downs of Elijah's, his companion on Mount Tabor. Attending to the lives of these men and these mountains made sense of my disillusionment and allowed me to welcome my apocalypse.

In the years since leaving local church ministry, I've devoted an enormous amount of time and resources to examining the church's often troubled witness, its ongoing crisis of leadership, and the epidemic of narcissism, abuse, and cover-up that has continued to emerge year after year. That examination led me to produce *The Rise and Fall of Mars Hill*, a podcast in which I attempted to document just one of many visible leadership collapses and the light it shines on a branch of the church that is image-conscious, charismatic, and contradictory.

This book is about the journey before and undergirding that work. The shattering of dreams and the grace that restored a broken faith in the aftermath. It's a story about grace leading me home when I thought all was lost.

In arriving here in a somewhat postapocalyptic place, I can see that remaining in the church wasn't a given. Like so many I know and love, I can easily imagine how my path into the void could have led somewhere other than here, back home. That strikes me as a tremendous mercy, and if there's any reason why I want to tell these stories, it's for a sense of gratitude for that grace.

Taken together, my encounters with Peter, Elijah, and Jesus connected to indelible images from my time in Israel and formed a new spiritual landscape in my mind, one with enough gravity to draw my feet back to solid ground. I still experience moments when I worry that I might sail off into space again. Like when you drive too quickly over a hill, there's a flash of that floating feeling where your stomach and feet seem to drift upward. Thankfully, each time that's happened, gravity and grace have brought my feet back to earth.

I hope that as I tell this story you might find echoes of your own. I pray if you're in the wilderness, you might find that though the territory is a mystery, you are far from alone. Most of all I pray that you rediscover that Jesus is chasing you like a lover—right through heaven's gates.

1

Mount Tabor

Light at the Summit
or *Glory at Mount Tabor*

The Hebrew calendar follows the cycle of the moon, not the sun, adjusting to follow its syncopated twenty-nine-and-a-half-day rhythm throughout the year—twenty-nine days this month, thirty days that one, and so on. The years expand and contract too. Some years add as much as a whole month.

The modern Hebrew calendar is calculated mathematically to ebb and flow over several years. Before that the beginning of a new month came at the first actual visual appearance of the new moon. When spotted, someone would send word to Jerusalem where religious leaders would confirm and announce the beginning of a new month.

At the sound of a shofar, according to the Mishnah, "they used to bring long poles of cedar and reeds and olive wood and flax fluff which they tied to the poles with a string, and someone used to go up to the top of a mountain and set fire to them and wave them to and fro and up and down until he saw the next one doing the same thing on the top of the second mountain; and so on the top of the third mountain" (Mishnah Rosh Hashanah 2:3).

You may have encountered something similar in *The Lord of the Rings: The Return of the King*. To summon aid, beacons are lit in Gondor and then from mountaintop to mountaintop, calling the men of Rohan to war. The message moves, more or less, at the speed of light.

For Jews the beginning of the month is known and celebrated as Rosh Chodesh, and while it's a minor holiday, it plays an important role—which is particular in the ancient Near East, where tracking the phases of the moon wasn't a precise art. By officially recognizing the new month centrally, in Jerusalem, it kept Jews throughout the diaspora in sync on high holy days—Purim on the fourteenth of Adar, Passover beginning on the fifteenth of Nisan, and so on.

Rosh Chodesh is also associated with resilience and renewal. From Abraham onward the Jewish people experienced seasons of flourishing and suffering, but just as the moon waxes, wanes, and returns, their survival has too. Like Rosh Chodesh itself, the flames of the beacons were symbols of hope and renewal passed from generation to generation, mountaintop to mountaintop.

Southwest of the Sea of Galilee and east of Nazareth is a mountaintop that is believed to have once been the site of such a beacon. Today, this alien-looking half-sphere that rises above the Jezreel Valley houses not one but two monasteries. In the first century the mountain was called Itabyrium. We know it today as Mount Tabor. And we remember it not because of the long-forgotten beacon but because of another event that took place here—another eruption of light that signaled a new beginning for God's people.

———— X ————

The first time I saw Mount Tabor I was just outside Nazareth on Mount Precipice, where an angry mob once tried to throw Jesus off the top of it. On the day I visited, the skies were a surreal, shimmering blue. Broad cumulus clouds hung in the distance, flattened atop warm air from the Jezreel Valley as though they were melting on glass. Mount Precipice isn't particularly high, but the valley is so flat and sprawling that the view gave me a sense of vertigo. Gideon battled the Amalekites at Jezreel, and it's been the site of wars ever since—as recently as the First World War.

When I stood on Mount Precipice, the Jezreel Valley stretched below, and Nazareth was to the right, stacked up the Galilean hills. Mount Tabor rose to my left, and I could immediately see why it would have made a perfect site for a beacon. It's what's known as an *inselberg* or an island mountain, the result of colliding fault lines driving a lone mound of rock up from the surface. Jeremiah saw its solitary, commanding presence as a metaphor for the coming of the Messiah, who would be "like Tabor among the mountains" (Jeremiah 46:18). Psalm 89 imagines Tabor as a singer, joining Mount Hermon to praise God. The choice of these two peaks isn't arbitrary; Hermon and

Tabor were contested spaces and scenes of desecration, "high places" where idolatry and evil infected the Holy Land and spread to the cities and valleys below them. The psalmist was reminding his listeners that God had staked his claim on these places, and they were meant for his worship.

It was about three years into Jesus' ministry. While the other disciples were in the town below, serving the crowds that had gathered because of Jesus' arrival, Peter, James, and John joined Jesus on a hike up Mount Tabor.

By now this trio had been established as Jesus' inner circle, and I wonder if their closeness to Jesus gave them some anticipatory sense that something was going to happen as they ascended the mountain. Nevertheless, when they reached the top, Jesus began to radiate white light, shining brighter and brighter until he became difficult to see. Then, suddenly, he was not alone. He was flanked by Moses and Elijah, talking with them like old friends.

Imagine living in a place where an evil empire has either crowded out or corrupted all of the spiritual and cultural values that you hold most dear. Imagine spending your entire life hearing stories about generations past, when similar crises of politics, culture, and spirituality had troubled your people until right was restored by mighty prophets and warriors. Imagine hearing that another warrior would come and do it again someday. Now before you two of these mighty men of old reappear alongside your rabbi, a man who you've seen command demons and perform countless healings, feed five thousand people, and walk on water. If there was any doubt in your mind that Jesus was going to carry the mantle of heroes past and lead a revolution to restore your people, it was gone now.

The place where this happens speaks volumes too. As mentioned, Mount Tabor overlooks the Jezreel Valley, which may be one of the most blood-soaked landscapes in human history. Contested again and again for its incredible fertility and its strategic importance. Through a mountain pass to the west lies the Mediterranean Sea and rich trade. Go north from Jezreel and you can get closer to the sea but you lose the fertile land. Go south and it's rocks and crags for miles. East is desert. Jezreel was a precious place.

Wars have been waged there since at least the fifteenth century BC, documented in the Hebrew Bible. In the stories of Deborah, Gideon, Saul, Jesu, and Josiah. Moses and Elijah themselves fought in it or for it as well. An ancient city sits in the pass to the sea like a gateway. Many of these wars converged on that city; control the pass and you control the immense wealth that can be cultivated in a wide swath of the Fertile Crescent. That town is known as Tel Megiddo. We derive the word *Armageddon* from that name.

Like the beacons lit at the start of the new month—notably the darkest part of the lunar cycle—Jesus' transfiguration into a beacon of light must have overwhelmed Peter, James, and John with the announcement of something new—a new season, a new hope for the people of God. Flanked by the prophet-warrior who conquered this land in the first place and another who later cleansed it of idolatry, no scene could confirm more deeply the hopes of Jews like these three men who longed to see Israel restored to its former glory. That restoration was their heart's desire. They'd anticipated it all their lives.

Peter seems to have been the first to find his words in this holy moment, and they rush out as if from a child who can't hide their feelings. I think Eugene Peterson gets at this best in his translation *The Message*: "Master, this is a great moment!" (Matthew 17:4).

The next sentence is the most revealing. "If you wish," Peter says, "I'll make three shelters for you."

Some see Peter's eagerness as a profound error. He's putting Moses and Elijah on level ground with Jesus. I'm skeptical of that interpretation. I don't think he's making a theological statement or judgment. While Peter is often impulsive, I think a better way to see him is guileless. He can't hide or contain what he's thinking and feeling. There's passion at his core, and it often takes the driver's seat.

So, Peter can hardly process the scene before him: the radiance of Jesus and the presence of these heroes of faith. All the while he feels minutes and seconds slipping between his fingers, feels the presence of the other disciples waiting below, feels the lingering shadow cast by Jesus' earlier prediction of his death.

"This is a holy moment," he says, desperate to make it last. "Let's set up camp."

It's a childlike request: "Can we just stay here?"

————X————

On September 11, 2000—a year before that date would become infamous in American history—I woke up to my phone ringing at about 7:30 in the morning. I was exhausted and sore from the combination of physical labor and stress that had filled the day before, and I wasn't happy about waking up.

On the other end of the line was my friend Jeremy. We'd been close for years having served in a variety of music ministries together at churches, camps, and retreats. We'd also played in a couple of bands together. Jeremy was a worship leader, and I was the music director at the time at Sojourn, a new church plant in Louisville, Kentucky. He'd been part of our core team for the first few months. His brother had been one of the founding pastors. But Jeremy left in February when his brother's marriage ended, wisely choosing to step back into his home church for some stability as they rallied around his brother and processed grief. We still were close friends—he was engaged to my wife's best friend; we just hadn't served in ministry together in a while.

"What are you doing?" he asked.

"Sleeping," I said.

"Can you meet me for breakfast?"

I was working as a barista at the time (planting a church does not a full-time salary make) but happened to have this particular morning off. "Sure. Where?"

"Dooley's Bagels?"

I agreed and got out of bed to head to the bakery. I was sore all over. The day before had been the second of two planned preview services for Sojourn, with the launch scheduled for next Sunday, September 17. We were renting an old church in the Highlands neighborhood in Louisville, and they were incredibly generous to us. Their sound system, though, wasn't prepared to handle the demands of a full band, and they had no available storage, so all of our speakers, amps, mics, drums, and instruments were down the road at an art gallery Sojourn had opened. In might sound unusual for a church plant to launch an art gallery ahead of regular services. It was, but that was who we were. In any event pulling off a Sunday service meant packing three to four truckloads of gear, hauling it a couple of miles down the street to Highland Baptist Church, loading it all in, calibrating it, rehearsing a band for a couple of hours, leading the service, then breaking it all down and hauling it back. The process started around noon, with a service at six, and we finished unloading back at the gallery around 10:00 p.m. We didn't have many hands on deck that particular weekend, thus the sore, tired body.

I was mentally exhausted too. This imminent launch stemmed from the almost chance meeting of a few different pockets of like-minded believers. Jeremy's brother had been a youth leader at a mainline Christian church in the area, but his students were having trouble feeling authentic (a big deal, especially to young people and especially in the late 1990s) in a rather straight-laced setting: wearing T-shirts of their favorite bands all week and putting on a polo and khakis for Sunday. The youth group made contact with another group of young believers coming out of Louisville's underground and punk scene and began dreaming up

22

a church that sounded and looked like them but was rooted in the gospel. The addition of an energetic church planter from the Southern Baptist seminary in town helped open doors. This church planter, the lead pastor, was a gifted speaker and had a way of rallying people, especially people who were hungry for something they could call their own. So, the Sojourn launch in September 2000 was the fruit of a lot of searching and a lot of hard work.

For the months leading up to the church's launch, we'd been struggling to figure out who our worship leader would be. I was music director but didn't sing. (I never have.) Jeremy left in February and another of our potential worship leaders left too. A third moved to Nashville. Another to Philly. That summer, a young guy showed up with his guitar to a Wednesday night Bible study and blew us away. He was a natural leader from the platform and drew out our little gathering into loud, joyful singing.

For the next several months he and I worked together on those Wednesday nights, choosing songs and talking about arrangements with the bands. By September 3 we were firing on all cylinders. The kid was naturally gifted to lead from the front, focused on the congregation and the singers who'd join him on stage. I was leading the band, dialing in arrangements, trying to push our sounds and ideas into creative territory that felt more like a native language to us. We'd established a musical fingerprint that was dark and reverent, which was a pretty stark departure from the sound of contemporary Christian worship we'd all grown up with but resonant with our hearts and sensibilities.

I think it's hard to overstate the importance of the musical shifts of the early 2000s to people who didn't live through it. The baby boomers had built churches that looked like casinos and convention centers, and the contemporary worship music that came from Orange County hippies in the 1970s had evolved into a highly polished genre all its own. The big hits at the time were songs like "Shout to the Lord" and "Shine Jesus Shine." It may have served its audience, but it was a radical disconnect for Gen Xers like me who were listening to the angsty rock of the 1990s. The previous generation had contextualized hymnody into their 1970s aesthetic. We were ready to take another leap.

To walk into a church in the year 2000 and find a room full of young people dressed mostly in black, with a stage full of candles and loud guitars, where the music was mostly in a minor key, was a serious dose of culture shock. But for people like me, it felt like we'd come home.

The day before Jeremy called me, our last preview service before launch had been a bit of a disaster. It began to unravel about midway through setup when I noticed our worship leader wasn't there.

I tried calling his house. I think maybe he had a pager, and I think I called it too. Thirty minutes passed. Call again. We started rehearsing the songs that another singer led. Called again. An hour late by this time. I started adapting the musical set and figuring out who else could sing. Cut this song. Change that key. The keyboard player sings this. Jen sings that. I even sang one myself. It was the only time in fifteen years I'd ever sing at a Sojourn service. No recordings exist. At quarter till, as people were making their way in, I finally made peace with the fact that the guy just wasn't coming.

It would be twelve years before I heard from him again. It turns out he went on to a successful music career. He moved to Nashville, was nominated for a Dove Award, and later became a worship leader at several large churches. We had a pretty good laugh about his disappearing act. We were all young—him especially—and God had done a lot of good in the intervening twelve years. But that preview service ended on an unsettling note. And then the phone rang the next morning and I headed to Dooley's Bagels.

I think of this story often because it reminds me of how easily things might have been different.

Jeremy and I sat in the dining room surrounded by the black-and-white checkered tile and the noisy morning crowd. He had an ear-to-ear grin and was excited that I saw in him, from time to time, a kind of childlike joy that I've always admired.

"I had a dream last night," he said.

"Okay," I said.

"Have you seen *Being John Malkovich*?"

Being John Malkovich—a wonderfully weird Charlie Kaufman–Spike Jonze film in which John Cusack discovers a portal into the actual John Malkovich's mind.

"So, in this dream, we all went to see Delirious."

Delirious is a British band that wrote and recorded a lot of the worship hits of the early 2000s, like "I Could Sing of Your Love Forever" and "Majesty."

"Okay," I said.

"And while they're playing, we get invited backstage after the show. Someone randomly gives us passes."

"All right."

"And we show up in this room backstage. And the band's there and other people are there and we're milling around, but it's super dull. There's just concrete floors and walls and the lighting's dim and there's a folding table with two-liter bottles and some bags of chips on it. And then suddenly someone points out this little door, hidden under the table."

"Like the portal in *Being John Malkovich*?"

"Precisely, and Martin Smith [from Delirious] is like, 'Let's see where this goes.' So, we all start lining up and crawling through the portal, and then it turns into a slide kind of thing, and we're all kind of falling through it, but it's not scary or anything. Everyone's excited. And then it dumps us out into this incredible mountain lake. There are cliffs all around us and the water is warm and the sun is shining, and it's just perfect. And we're all astonished too. Like, we know how weird it is that we've been transported there. And people keep saying things like, 'Can you believe this is here?' And 'How did we get here?'"

Jeremy's not the most charismatic person in the world, and by *charismatic* I mean prone to this sort of vision or dream, or to speaking in tongues or anything that one would be tempted to call prophecy in the contemporary sense. At the same time we were all kind of charismatic-adjacent then (and maybe still are) because of experiences we'd had as worship leaders. While this sort of conversation wasn't an everyday occurrence for us, it also wasn't something either of us would have greeted with total bewilderment.

"So, we're swimming around," he said, "and at some point Martin Smith comes up out of the water right in front of me, and he looks me in the eyes and he says, 'Can you believe we almost missed this?' And I woke up on the spot and just knew, in my core, that I needed to come back to Sojourn."

This memory is funny to me. It's vivid, though I'm not sure it felt like a powerful moment at the time. It was just kind of interesting—more of a *hmm, okay* moment than a *wow*. But I also didn't have any doubt about any of it. Jeremy is one of the most honest and sincere people I've ever met. A sense of calm settled in me. A feeling of confidence that things were unfolding exactly the way they were supposed to.

We launched our first official service as a church that following Sunday. In the years that followed, Jeremy and I have led more worship services together than we could count, and he's written and recorded dozens of songs. Sojourn Music never became a household name, but we did connect to a broader movement of church-based music that would emerge in the next decade. Because of that, Jeremy's songs are sung in hundreds of churches across the country and in the United Kingdom, New Zealand, and Australia.

I can remember on that first Sunday, in particular, singing a brooding version of Michael Pritzl's "Light of the World." Jeremy and I had probably played it a hundred times before in various settings, but that night it felt different. There was something new about the way the snare drum and the reverb-drenched electric guitars echoed off the limestone. Candles flickered off windows depicting prophets, apostles, and saints from church history. This stained-glass cloud of witnesses surrounded about seventy-five people, almost all wearing black T-shirts or hoodies. Some sang. Some scowled. Some stood cross-armed with the same stoic cool I'd seen on their faces at indie rock shows in crappy venues around town. But they were here. A gang of punk rock ragamuffins who'd felt out of place at most of the churches we'd attended. We'd found a home.

We named the church Sojourn, a nod to a song by the poster child of ragamuffins, Rich Mullins. It was born out of deep friend-ships, years of wandering, and months of intense work and prayer. We worshiped together in a shared cultural language, as though our liturgy had finally been translated from Latin to our native tongue. Music was key—an aesthetic that tied us together—but there was so much more. Something in seed form that I imagine is what theologian Dietrich Bonhoeffer meant when he talked about the spirit of a beloved community.

I still feel a part of my heart clench when I think of the light in that darkened room in the early years of the church. I can close my eyes and find myself there instantly. See the candles casting flickering shadows. Feel the creaking of the wooden floors. Hear the whispered prayers and the music. I understand why these kinds of experiences are often referred to as mountaintops. They elevate the soul.

I completely understand Peter's response there at the top of Mount Tabor. When you encounter glory, you desperately want to make it last.

Can we just stay here?

2

Mount Carmel and the Hope of Heroes

Seekers, pilgrims, and hermits have sought Carmel Ridge for centuries. This high curtain of limestone and flint, pockmarked by caves and narrow hollows, sits about forty-five miles west of Mount Tabor, marking the western border of the Jezreel Valley. Long ago one of the peaks was known as Mount Carmel. Roughly one thousand years before he appeared on Mount Tabor alongside Jesus, Elijah confronted evil in a way that resonates inside Judaism, Christianity, and Islam to this day.

It was a dark time for Israel. The people had abandoned their God and taken up the Canaanite worship of Baal and Asherah, the god of power, and his wife, the goddess of fertility. Unlike what we often call paganism today, worshipers of Baal and Asherah weren't wearing crystals, smoking weed, and dancing with glow sticks at a Phish concert. No, these gods presided over a violent and coercive blood-and-sex cult. The demands of Baal worship required ever-increasing sacrifices, including the lives of children. And Asherah not only permitted but required all manner of sexual deviancy, including prostitution and what we would today call human trafficking.

This predatory religion had captured the spiritual imaginations of the people and enslaved the kingdom, and the nation was growing evermore bloody and corrupt. Just before Elijah appears in 1 Kings 18, the author tells the story of Hiel of Bethel, who rebuilt Jericho. When he laid the foundation of the city, he sacrificed his oldest son. When he finished its gates, he sacrificed his youngest. Anointing a city so central to Israel's story of rescue and deliverance to the Promised Land with the blood of children marked the bottom of a deep valley.

In his translation of verses immediately following Hiel's story, Eugene Peterson writes: "And then this happened: Elijah the Tishbite . . . confronted Ahab" (1 Kings 17:1 MSG).

And then this happened.

Ahab hails Elijah, the "Troubler of Israel," and Elijah indeed brings trouble, informing the king that there would be no more rain in the land. It was a kind of holy middle finger to Baal, who supposedly controlled thunder, lightning, and, notably, rain. Elijah was right, and the ensuing drought brought the king to his knees.

After three dry years, Elijah appears again, challenging Ahab to gather all of the priests of Baal and meet him at Mount Carmel.

Four hundred and fifty prophets of Baal show up along with another four hundred prophets of Asherah. A crowd of Israelites gathers as well—probably on the plain below the Carmel Ridge, where the events would be visible.

Elijah presents straightforward terms: you build an altar, and I'll build an altar, we'll both ask our gods to consume our sacrifices, and we'll see what happens. The prophets of Baal go first. They yell and shout from morning to noon. Nothing happens. The prophets start cutting themselves with swords and lances, soaking themselves and their altar with their blood. The author of 1 Kings writes flatly: "No one answered, no one paid attention" (1 Kings 18:29).

Elijah's turn. We're told he restores an altar to the Lord on the mountain. This is scandalous; the proper altar to Israel's God is in the temple in Jerusalem, and there's not supposed to be more than one at any given time. The author of 1 Kings tells us Elijah is "rebuilding" or "restoring" this altar, which could mean that there was an older altar here, before the construction of the temple in Jerusalem (v. 30). It certainly emphasizes renewal. The temple had been utterly defiled along with the rest of Israel. Elijah's rebuilt altar invites a long-overdue purge of spiritual and religious corruption.

Elijah builds his altar with twelve stones representing the twelve tribes of Israel. After assembling the stones, he proceeds to dig a trench and orders the whole thing doused with four jars of water three times—twelve jars total. The act is liturgical, a kind of performance art that visualizes the purification needed in Israel. Before calling out to the Lord to consume the offering, he lays on top of it and prays. When Elijah rises, fire falls from heaven, consuming the offering, the altar itself, and the water in the trenches. The gathered crowd falls to their faces like Peter before the transfiguration, confessing "The LORD—he is God" (v. 39). Elijah then drives the prophets of Baal down the cliffs to the valley below. All are killed.

Such a massacre is unpleasant to most modern ears, but understand who these priests were: profiteers of exploitation, ritualized murder, and sex trafficking. The point of the story and their destruction is as much symbolic as practical. Their religion and corruption had to be ripped from the kingdom stem to root. Their deaths are both an act of judgment and a work of redemption, a new exodus from a different kind of oppression.

Elijah returns to King Ahab and tells him the drought is over. A cloud appears like the hand of God rising from the sea, expanding and turning the sky black. Rain returned to the thirsty plains of Jordan.

This is the Elijah Peter saw talking with Jesus atop Mount Tabor. Bringer of heavenly fire, mocker of idols, and vanquisher of their prophets. A true lightning rod for the awe-striking power of God. I can easily picture Peter looking from Elijah to Jesus and back and starting to imagine what might be coming.

Like Peter, I had many Elijahs in the background of my spiritual imagination. Renowned men of God famous for their impact. I grew up watching the ministry of Billy Graham, saw the rise of Bill Hybels and Rick Warren, played guitar in churches that were fighting the worship wars, and watched bands like DC Talk and Jars of Clay become cultural forces to reckon with both inside and outside the church. Jerry Falwell and James Dobson were heroes in my home. My parents' churches supported (and sometimes led) the conservative resurgence in the Southern Baptist Convention— a reversal of decades of theological drift. I walked aisles to dedicate and rededicate my faith, was part of trust falls and games of chubby bunny, took part in events with names like Megaworship, saw holy laughter and holy barking up close, signed purity pledges, and considered kissing dating goodbye.

It's a popular pastime to crap on this evangelical culture from a great height, and some of that critique is necessary. But some of it is a revisionist oversimplification, and we need to resist caricature if we want to avoid repeating old mistakes just with new blind spots of our own.

The generation that came before us made laudable strides for the church. Evangelicalism emerged as a middle way between two drifts: a leftward drift informed by modernity and its propensity to deconstruct all truth claims, and a rightward drift toward an ever-more-narrowing fundamentalism.

Evangelicals saw their world changing and understood the church needed to be engaged in the social and cultural issues that would shape the twentieth century. But they also wanted to hold on to the historic convictions of Protestantism. Their movement offered a third way that attempted to draw out faithful practices from both liberals and fundamentalists. And no one embodied bridge building more than Billy Graham.

Graham demonstrated a transformational vision for Christianity that remained committed to the inerrancy of Scripture and motivated by evangelism yet demonstrated a generosity of spirit that looked different from moralistic, fire-and-brimstone fundamentalism. He became an omnipresent spokesperson for the movement with televised "crusades," media appearances, and a role as America's pastor that saw him counseling presidents and heads of state.

Like anyone, his record isn't unblemished. But overall his life and ministry were marked by integrity. His place in the popular imagination set the standard—and the high expectations, especially surrounding access to power and having a seat at the table—for those who would follow him. Still, unlike many who followed in his footsteps to stardom, Billy Graham didn't want your money; he wanted to save your soul.

Mark Noll once said that the best definition of an evangelical was someone who likes Billy Graham. I count myself among them.

But let me also tell you about my grandfather Sam Cooley.

Sam Cooley joined the Marines at eighteen and fought in the Pacific theater of World War II. After the war, he started his family and went to work for Eastern Airlines as a mechanic. Before the civil rights movement had begun cracking at the hard conscience of White America, Sam saw the effects of segregation in the lives of his Black coworkers. Men who'd served in the war and had come home to shuttle White passengers to and from the same airports that wouldn't let them, as Black men, in the door. My grandfather would make a space for them in the hangars, getting them a meal from inside the airport when he could. He didn't make a show of it. I doubt he thought of himself as a radical. He was just being decent and neighborly, especially to those who'd served their country in a time of crisis.

Sam worked as a decision counselor at his church and Billy Graham rallies, greeting those who'd walked the aisle to become Christians and preparing them to get baptized or find a church. If you met him at a hardware store—where you'd often find him— he'd want to know all about you. He'd especially want to know if you knew Jesus and whether he could introduce you to him.

Sam's kids—my mom and uncles—grew up in churches where they were encouraged to participate in ministries that might have scandalized others my grandfather's age. They weren't part of the Jesus movement, but like many Christians in the 1970s they were part of the evangelical culture that emerged from it, embracing contemporary Christian music, the modernization of church culture, and the work of writers and evangelists like Josh McDowell and Francis Schaeffer.

For Sam, who every Sunday wore a suit, a clean shave, and a haircut that would have passed military inspection, I'm sure some of the cultural shifts inside the church were deeply uncomfortable. But like Graham and many other evangelical leaders in the 1960s and 1970s, he didn't see these changes as threatening. So long as the gospel maintained its place at the heart, you could pick up a guitar or wear a golf shirt. His clean-cut military bearing gave him a conservative air, but he wasn't concerned about politics or misogyny or protecting White supremacy (and to be sure, some were at the time—including some in his own church and denomination). No, like Billy Graham, he didn't want your power or your money; he wanted to save your soul.

There were Elijahs in the generations before mine. Some, like Billy Graham, loomed large in the newly televised American culture and brought a lot of fame to the church. Some, like my grandfather, lived quiet, faithful lives, raising families, helping neighbors, and trying to introduce people around them to their Savior. The bright lights of fame can often outshine such smaller—at least in terms of scale—acts of ministry. I am certain many people were drawn to Graham because they needed to find Jesus. And others moved into evangelicalism because they wanted fame.

The word *evangelical* is complicated today. It has evolved into a sort of catchall for a certain kind of White religious voter—something that didn't begin with Trump. I remember objecting to that usage as far back as 2004, when it served as a broad scare word to warn those on the left of the voters that wanted the theocratic government George W. Bush would certainly install if reelected. On this path *evangelical* ended up representing most any voter with even nominal conservative religious associations, whether they're Protestant, Catholic, churchgoing, or not. This framing, though, creates weird divisions. For example, it excludes many people of color who might consider themselves evangelical in their religious convictions but who wouldn't vote for the GOP. And it puts people like me, a White American male, in uneasy company, sharing a common label with others who might say they're Christian but don't share my conviction that a big part of the Christian life is active membership in a local body. This politicized reframing of evangelicalism doesn't represent the actual values and origins of the evangelical movement. Despite the protests of politicians and pundits who want to make it so to baptize their platform.

Maybe the word *evangelical* itself needs to go. (I think it does.) But if that's the case, we need to be cautious not to throw the baby out with the bathwater. Again, yes, there's a lot about evangelical culture to critique. And there's no doubt that the measure of fame, respectability, and influence achieved by some in the movement attracted a parade of manipulative, corrupted, and abusive leaders whose various unmaskings have dominated the news in the last decade. But when we let them represent the entire evangelical movement, we lose sight of men and women like Billy Graham and Sam Cooley.

They and others occupied a large place in my imagination. Billy Graham might have been an icon, but Sam Cooley was the one who would show up to a Sojourn worship service or to my front door with a few bucks so my wife and I could go out for a date during the leanest years of ministry. Then there are people like Philip Yancey and Dallas Willard, who showed me a Jesus whose depths weren't just theological, they were personal. Max Lucado made the people in the Bible seem human. Corrie ten Boom showed me what it meant to be light in the darkness. Rick Warren taught me to think about how my neighbor saw the world. Steve Taylor taught me to laugh at hypocrisy and folly both inside and outside the church.

There were many others, including some who now evoke sadness for the wounds and damage they were causing out of the public eye. This is one of the most complicated elements of our faith; the very people who can help us meet and know Jesus are also the ones who can hurt us at the deepest levels.

Mark Driscoll is certainly one of these characters. For all the discussion about the fall of Driscoll's Seattle church, Mars Hill, in the podcast *The Rise and Fall of Mars Hill*, I truly tried to show why the church rose in the first place. Driscoll inspired many men and women to be unapologetic about their faith, even in environments like Seattle, where Christianity was seen as arcane or oppressive. He was known for a kind of private and personal generosity to pastors who were struggling or burned out. My interactions with him were few. I met him only three times. But each time was marked by kindness. With no other context I would likely have felt the same cognitive dissonance others felt when, in 2013 and 2014, horror stories began to emerge about life inside Mars Hill.

Others could tell similar stories about other fallen leaders, from Bill Hybels to Jean Vanier to James MacDonald. No one is just one thing, even the worst of us. That doesn't excuse anyone's behavior, but it does complicate a narrative we might otherwise want to make very simple.

——X——

Evangelicalism—like every social or religious movement before or since—wanted to present itself as a standard-bearer for virtue. Highly visible and influential leaders like Billy Graham gave rise to Elijah-level expectations: that a Christian society could win over the increasing sexual liberation and increasing social acceptability of drug use that seemed to loom large, and that incentivized all kinds of institutions to prop up their leaders as moral mascots. A variety of other factors—some implicitly adopted from a culture of entrepreneurship, some evolving naturally out of an emphasis on evangelism, and some emerging from the sinful heart's longing for glory—also incentivized those institutions to think about growth at all costs. The fruit we see bearing out today, though, is far from what we expected or hoped.

In the light of a decade's worth of scandals, in the upheaval of the Trump years, the temptation for many has been to throw the entire concept of evangelicalism to the curb along with the leaders who hurt and failed us. And the movement itself helped foster the expectations that have led to such bitter resentment.

But we bear some responsibility as well. They were our expectations, after all. We want heroes and want to be heroes. We imagine ourselves as the Billy Grahams, the Elijahs. We like to imagine ourselves in their company. We want to be that effective. To shape a society where our set of values and preferences is the norm. Where we can fit in and not be troubled. But we are in grave danger if avoiding being troubled becomes a goal. Once we begin telling ourselves that story, it becomes easier to ignore troubling warning signs in our leaders. In what they do and how they treat the people around them while on mission. Our high expectations can lead us to overlook—maybe even kind of want to overlook—symptoms of unhealth or evidence of character flaws that could prove fatal.

As a result our version of Mount Carmel dominates our spiritual landscape, eclipsing other mountains, valleys, and deserts that are soaked with blood and tears. We see Elijah, the fire from heaven, and the defeated prophets, and we tell ourselves this is our future. That our victory is coming in this world. And we repeat the story to drown out any misgivings that would otherwise warn us: *you might just have this one wrong.* We're helped along the way by an evangelical culture that incentivizes and reinforces that story and by a broader American culture that continually hungers for celebrities and heroes.

I'm not sure there's a great defense against it at the moment. I'm not sure you can go out into the world, green and ambitious, and simultaneously have the inner wisdom to avoid being seduced by the tendency to tell ourselves the stories we want to hear, to resist propping up our heroes so they tower like saints. In some ways we need heroes. And sometimes the hero is real. But Mount Carmel is only half the story for Elijah just as victory is only half the story for most heroes.

The fundamental arc of the Christian story does not ascend from glory to glory. It bends to the cross. In denying that we, like Peter, might overlook the occasionally drawn sword—we may even draw a sword of our own—to protect the mission. And others among us may be on the receiving end of true harm. And, like Peter, when we finally see our expectations starting to crumble, we can find ourselves in denial. A choice lies before us. Stick with the falling hero or let go and enter the darkness of true reflection, accountability, and lament over what happened in our midst. While I don't know if failure is avoidable, I don't think it's a mistake we have to repeat. But we must be willing to bend—to bow, really—and learn.

The alternative is to keep the plotline front of mind and keep putting one foot in front of the other. It's hard to get out of bed if you know that your dreams are cracking, so you cling to the story that still looks like Mount Carmel. You look for reasons to believe you're still on the side of Moses, Jesus, and Elijah. And you cling with all your might to every glimmer of confirmation that this story is still true.

Can we just stay here?

3

Mount Hermon and the Dreams We Dream

Israel, Syria, and Lebanon intersect at a mountainous stretch of land known as the Golan Heights. It's made up, in part, of the western edge of territory known in the Bible as Bashan, a place of conflict for Israel from the moment Moses led the tribe into the Promised Land and faced war with King Og. It's been contested ever since, including in 1967, during the Six-Day War.

For the Bible's first readers a reference to Bashan evoked power, strength, and menace: the towering oaks of Bashan mentioned by both Isaiah and Ezekiel or the bulls of Bashan threatening to rip the psalmist to pieces in Psalm 22, which Jesus quotes from the cross.

In modern times, approaching from the south, from the vibrant and fertile Jezreel Valley and the rolling green hills of Galilee, you pass lush vineyards and orchards growing on kibbutzim that were established by Zionist settlers in the late nineteenth and early twentieth centuries. As you drive further north, the landscape changes. Craggy limestone formations emerge like teeth. The rich green fades, with patches of scrubby brown and green brush appearing in bursts along the side of the road. The ground begins to rise toward Mount Hermon, and the foothills are full of sinkholes and yawning caves. One of those caves is especially forbidding. It feels haunted, like the gaping maw of some terrible creature.

The Canaanites once controlled this land and made that cave a centerpiece of their pagan religion. Because its internal temperature was constant throughout the year, they believed that the gods who inhabited the region would retreat into the cave during the cold months. The land had passed through many hands before Canaan's and has passed through many others since.

Today, it is a part of modern Israel, and it remains an attractive place for pagan practice. When I visited in 2015 there was a gathering of Americans who would have looked at home in a graduate seminar on cryptozoology or a Grateful Dead concert. Men and women alike had shaggy, shoulder-length hair and wore coronas made of flowers or olive leaves. A shoeless blonde woman played Joan Baez on an acoustic guitar. She was accompanied by a man in late middle age with a pan flute. Something vaguely and uncomfortably resembling dancing was taking place. One sensed the presence of hallucinogens. Incense scented the air, and as the smoke rose in the breeze, some incantation about earth and wind wafted by.

Once again, this kind of hippy paganism bears little resemblance to the blood-soaked paganism practiced in antiquity.

In the first century the land was under Roman rule. Like the Persians and Babylonians before them, they had the habit of appropriating local religions and adding their gods and practices to their pantheon. This cave had been adopted and dedicated to the worship of Pan. Around it a city had grown up—a busy crossroads of the empire with a bathhouse, a marketplace, and temples devoted to both Zeus and Pan. Get any technicolor image of noblemen in togas out of your head: the place probably operated much more like the world of *The Sopranos*—a complex intersection of religion, sex, money, politics, commerce, and criminality. Welcome to Caesarea Phillipi.

The temple to Pan sat directly in front of the cave. Worshipers and priests sacrificed animals in front of it and tossed the carcasses into the darkness. A spring running out of the mouth of the cave flowed past the temple and out into the city below. If Pan accepted the sacrifice, the water ran clean. If not, the animal's blood would stain it, a sign that the god was unsatisfied and demanding more. A common name for this dark and bloody place? The Gates of Hell.

Jesus and his disciples arrived here at the foot of Mount Hermon just a few months before Mount Tabor. Their experience here is important, providing some key insight into exactly what Peter had seen—or wanted to see—in the brilliant miracle at the peak of that other mountain.

For more than six hundred years Israel had been conquered territory. Jews like Peter felt the presence of occupation in their bones. We know from a later scene in the Gospels that Peter sometimes carried a sword, and I'd guess he wasn't the only one. Another disciple was known as Simon the Zealot. Zealots were radicals, openly rejecting the legitimacy of Roman rule and looking forward to the day Caesar could be overthrown. Having a friend named Simon the Zealot would be like having someone in your group of friends named Simon the Insurrectionist. If you had to place a bet on which of your friends had stormed the US Capitol on January 6 (albeit for a much less noble cause), you'd bet on him every time.

Sympathies for this point of view went well beyond the Zealots, though. Since the exodus, Jewish identity always involved the sense that Israel had the right and destiny of self-rule. It's a desire that stretched back to God's covenant with Abraham, a belief that this Promised Land was going to be the home of a kingdom that would endure forever. But of course it didn't. Sin and idolatry sent the kingdom spiraling into decay, weakening it and leading to its defeat against a Babylonian invasion. The Holy City fell, the ruling class was taken into captivity along with a large portion of the population, and the nation as a whole was humiliated. Years later, when they were given the right to return to their city, rebuild its walls, and restore their temple, they did so as subjects of the Persians. Subjugation had been the status quo ever since.

Peter dreamed of the day when Israel's sovereignty would be restored, and the story of Elijah was no small part of that dream. The word *prophet* has been neutered for most of us, associated primarily with either a kind of mystical fortune-telling or with the antics of televangelists sweating, shouting, and making glorious promises about their churches and the health and wealth of their people. Either description would have been wholly alien to Elijah, who only told the future in the sense that he spoke as a voice of God's judgment and foreshadowed the doom that would consume unrepentant idolators. In all of Israel's history the only person who had worked greater wonders and stunned audiences more was Moses. That is, until Jesus.

By the time Jesus arrived at Caesarea Philippi, he had performed countless miracles, casting out demons, healing the sick, multiplying loaves and fishes, walking on water, and calming storms. He had also spoken with audacity and authority to religious leaders.

Peter and the other disciples witnessed all of this and had begun to wonder if Jesus was not only the next great prophet in a continuum but also something more. The Scriptures had promised one who would come after Elijah who would not only restore Israel and cleanse it of its idols but also establish an even greater kingdom. He would be King of kings and Lord of lords—an emperor with authority and power like the world had never seen, and his kingdom would never end. Could Jesus be this Messiah?

I do not doubt that Peter was, at some level, drawn to Jesus and to the kingdom of heaven out of self-interested ambition. We all have an appetite for power. But there were other paths to power in Rome and Israel, and if that were all Peter wanted, he might have found more immediate paths than wandering up and down the countryside with the son of a carpenter. That's why I'm not compelled by many of the shorthand descriptions for Peter we find in books and sermons—the brash, jump-to-conclusions guy. Something more is going on.

Imagine yourself in Peter's shoes after these years of following Jesus. All the things you've seen. Some of the things you have done. You arrive in Caesarea Philippi immediately confronted by all that's wrong in Israel. Architecture that testifies to the greatness of Rome and its gods. Temples and bathhouses where bodies are exchanged in sexual transactions to please empty idols, not to mention pleasing the members of society who can afford them. Behind it all stands this cave—a center of Canaanite worship in years past, repurposed in Roman fashion but nonetheless a stain on this land you love.

Mount Hebron is significant in the narrative arc of the gospel, not because of a particular event that happened there but rather because of a conversation. Here, amid this stained land, arguably in the most flagrant defiance of the God of Israel, Jesus asks the disciples what people think about the Son of Man—a term he uses for himself (Matthew 16).

First, Peter gives a rundown of the rumors. Maybe John the Baptist or Elijah or another prophet. But you get the sense that Peter is dancing around something. Hedging.

"Who do you say I am?" Jesus asks. Not them. You, Peter.

"You are the Messiah," Peter says, "the Son of the living God" (vv. 15-16).

Peter finally says out loud what must have been rolling around in his head for months. It's a moment that shapes who I think Peter really is. Peter isn't just ambitious because, again, who on earth would think of wandering the countryside with a pauper as a ladder to success? He has stuck around too long to be merely curious about Jesus. He isn't chasing power for himself, and he isn't merely wondering what crazy thing Jesus will do next. He wants to believe. Jesus is the Messiah; Peter's dreams and the dreams of his fathers are coming true.

He isn't seduced by the sense that power awaits him. Peter is a true believer.

We thought we'd conquer the world. Most people thought we were crazy.

Imagine being a church-planting coordinator for a network or a denomination and our group walks through the door: a few not-yet-graduated seminary students with little to no professional ministry experience, a bunch of eighteen, nineteen, and twenty-something baristas, college students, and unemployed artists and musicians. You ask what our strategy is. We say we are launching an art gallery and music venue. You ask what kinds of Christian art and music we'd show. We say we aren't focusing on Christian art or music. The gallery will focus on local contemporary fine artists. Secular artists? Yes, of course. The music venue will focus on Louisville's indie rock scene. You ask about our evangelism strategy with the gallery and venue. We say we don't have one; that isn't the point. And what, then, is the point? We tell you about how we exist to *cultivate beauty* and show how we are *created for community*.

All of that was true—we really believed it. Perhaps a more direct answer would have been to simply say, "This is just what we're into." But we planted our church largely because our friends who didn't know Jesus were deeply suspicious of sometimes ham-handed ways churches tried to appear relevant to young people. Because the altar call would sound before any real relationship had been forged. Our gambit was that if we made space for people who loved music and art as much as we did and cultivated community with them, opportunities would come to share the gospel in a much less forced way. It all came back to authenticity.

Those early years at the church were truly wild. We were in the heart of an urban neighborhood and people would regularly walk in off the street drunk or high or otherwise out of their minds, pacing up and down the aisle, gesturing (dancing?) frantically during the music, whispering or shouting at demons. We never quite knew which side of the demons they were on. We tried to practice our faith. Homeless kids would get saved and people would move them into their spare bedrooms or attics, occasionally with disastrous results.

But we also were a community marked by deep friendships and deep commitments to one another. I have memory after memory of community group gatherings in homes where people laid bare their struggles with mental health, brittle marriages, or lifelong wounds; people gathered close, wept, prayed, and in many cases created support structures.

The art gallery became a well-respected spot for emerging artists in the city, many of whom would go on to show at higher-end galleries in the city and beyond. And since Louisville had no all-ages music venues at the time, our small stage (like Mars Hill's venue, The Paradox) met a need and flourished as a result.

April of each year was Kill Your TV/Cultivate Beauty Month, and we kicked it off with a service full of flowers that ended by gathering in the church parking lot to smash old TVs with sledgehammers and baseball bats. One year the celebration opened with a video filmed by church members in which old TVs were obliterated with a variety of handguns and an AK-47. Welcome to Kentucky.

I don't think I can overstate the sense of connection we felt. We were singing to Jesus in our own musical language, we were hearing Sojourn's lead pastor and others preach sermons with illustrations as likely to come from *The Simpsons* or *Seinfeld* as anything. The gospel truly came alive in the native language of our culture, and it bound us fast to one another. We were home. Our dream was coming true.

Nonetheless, people were often confused. Pastors and older Christians in town would hear about what we were doing and drive in to check it out, only to leave with more questions than they came with. Why was the music so loud? Why so many depressing songs? Why so much talk about death? Why was the sermon so long? Was that guy wearing a skirt, or was it a quilt? Not a kilt—that was the other guy. And why was everybody dressed in black? Was that a pair of six-shooters tattooed on the neck of the guy that served us Communion?

For the first three or four years Sojourn survived with denominational support and generosity from a handful of outside donors, but observers and advisers always asked us the same question: "How are you going to be self-supporting?" At the time the question infuriated us. How could anyone look into that room full of skaters, recovering drug addicts, wannabe rock stars, and college students, and doubt for a second that it was built to last?

I can laugh at the improbability of it all now. It's partially what Linford and Karin Detweiler of Over the Rhine call the laugh of recognition, "when you laugh but you feel like dyin'." It was a laugh born of the painful lesson that in many ways our church wasn't built to last. At least not in the way we thought.

But it's also the laughter of Abraham and Sarah when they heard they'd have a child—the laughter of astonishment that says, "Who but God?" (Genesis 18). I imagine their laughter didn't stop with that announcement. I imagine it likely reappeared at all of the childhood milestones. When Isaac spoke his first words, first toddled around their homestead or spoke like children do with eagerness and innocence at the world around him. I imagine Abraham laughed a lot when he and Isaac hiked back down Mount Moriah, having just found a ram in a thicket sparing the life of his son (Genesis 22). The laugh of relief and surprise; "Who but God?"

The laugh of recognition and the laugh of astonishment are intertwined for me. Astonishing things happened at Sojourn, not only for me but also for the marriages, lives, and souls saved at the church. The people who found faith—who are still finding faith in the churches that exist today because of Sojourn. I was privileged to witness it and take part in it.

I think that sense of astonishment and attendant gratitude probably commingles with pain in the hearts of many who live today with wounds from the spiritual communities they once (and still) loved. Whether it was Sojourn or Mars Hill or Willow Creek or Harvest Bible Chapel or Hillsong—any church where members and leaders had encounters with profound brokenness—there was beauty in its midst. God met people and changed lives despite it all.

4

The Mount of Olives and the Specter of Triumph

The road up the Mount of Olives is almost entirely hairpin turns on narrow streets. They were hair-raising to navigate even in a small car, but today, like every day, countless tour buses navigate them with ease. I felt a little less at ease, but we made it. From the top I had a panoramic view of the city of Jerusalem—the view you've probably seen in a hundred photos and news reports, the modern high rises of the past century in the distance, the golden Dome of the Rock gleaming above the old city.

The topography was deceptive. The Mount of Olives wasn't that much higher than the city itself, but when I stood at one of the overlooks, the earth plunged into the Kidron Valley, rising again at the Temple Mount. The valley teemed with tens of thousands of bone-white limestone tombs, slightly larger than a coffin. The world's largest Jewish cemetery, containing the graves of one hundred thousand or more people, sprawled across the valley almost as far as I could see.

When originally constructed, the eastern wall of the temple—the wall visible from the Mount of Olives—also served as the city wall of Jerusalem itself. Squared battlements run along the top of it, and a gatehouse juts out near its northeastern end. You can still see the twin arches from the doors that once led into the city, but the entrance is sealed. It's known by two names: the Golden Gate or the Mercy Gate, and it's been the subject of controversy for centuries.

Depending on who you read, the Golden Gate served one of a variety of purposes. Some say it was where the priests led the red heifer into the temple for a sacrifice. Others say it was where the scapegoat was led out of the temple. Still others say it was an entrance exclusively for the high priest.

Since the Middle Ages, Jewish tradition has held that this would be the gate the Messiah would use when entering Jerusalem. Of course, in the Christian tradition that entry happened two thousand years ago, when Jesus came to the city in the last week of his life.

In the months between the transfiguration and the triumphal entry, Jesus continued predicting his death. Peter had learned enough from being told "get behind me, Satan," at Mount Hermon (Matthew 16:23), to stop objecting out loud, but that doesn't mean he'd accepted his Teacher's death as a reality.

Preachers and commentary writers often posit that the disciples didn't comprehend what Jesus was telling them about his destiny when he came to Jerusalem. Jesus was cryptic, they say, and the disciples didn't understand. I think the reality is more straight-forward—Jesus wasn't cryptic at all in speaking of his death. Simple denial is much easier than to believe the incomprehensible.

Denial is a hell of a drug. Oceans of ink have been spilled describing how denial of death exists at the very root of the human experience, but denial isn't only about things we fear. It can also spring from what we cannot bear. Denial is the first of the stages of grief, and in experiences like Peter's—an experience that will soon unravel into the crushing loss of a dream—denial plays a major role.

This isn't to say that some measure of confusion isn't also at play. Jesus' ultimate purpose is to subvert our idea of what triumph is and by doing so reveal a new way of thinking about power, weakness, and the life men and women long for. To do so, he embraces the language of Elijah and Moses, speaking in parables that are often apocalyptic, describing a conquering kingdom in ways that would have been familiar to the peoples of the ancient Near East.

The triumphal entry is the ultimate appropriation of the imagery of a conquering emperor. This embrace peaks at the Mount of Olives. Jesus begins the last week of his life with a victory parade into the city he's conquered. Albeit he does so with a bit of a wink.

There are cheering crowds. There are songs. The air is thick with a mix of anticipation and joy. Palm branches wave like the banners of the new monarchy. But Jesus arrives not on a warhorse but on a donkey—the foal of a donkey at that. Horses were somewhere between the BMW and the Humvee of the day, at once a luxury vehicle and a fast-moving weapon of war. The donkey was a

Toyota, and the foal of the donkey was a Toyota Corolla. Following behind Jesus comes not an army but his disciples, a ragamuffin mix of tax collectors, blue-collar workers, and women.

It's an act of performance art, a parody of the victory parade. A joke that maybe only a few people (other than Jesus) fully appreciated at the time.

Maybe the clearest sign that *triumph* is the wrong word appears in Luke's account. As Jesus approaches the gates, he began to weep. He knew the time was coming when the Romans would once and for all put down any hope of a restoration of the kingdom of Israel, sacking the city and destroying the temple. "They will not leave one stone on another," he said, "because you did not recognize the time of God's coming to you" (Luke 19:44).

I've wondered whether Peter was standing nearby as Jesus said those words. Did he hear it? Did he feel the cognitive dissonance of the crowd's enthusiasm against the tears of grief pouring down Jesus' face? Or was it all drowned out by the noise around them and the noise in his own heart—the noisy dream that he couldn't let go?

We see what we want to see. Easier to cherry-pick reality than watch a dream die.

For the better part of a decade, Sojourn's story seemed enchanted. If you read many of the stats on church planting in the United States, you know that the failure rate is enormously high. We were one of the lucky ones, by the skin of our teeth able to not only survive but also thrive.

In the first five years our growth was slow, and our sense of mission was ever-evolving. One of the attractive things about church planting is also one of its liabilities—that you build the thing without much in the way of guardrails. So, as we tried to figure out what worked for the church, we ended up adopting different vision statements, catch phrases, member's agreements, and philosophies of ministry that might focus from season to season on community groups, evangelism, or the church gathering. Around 2005 I remember Sojourn's lead pastor and I were seriously considering throwing in the towel on vocational ministry, not because it was hard or daunting but because we weren't sure that the whole artifice of church planting and pastoring made sense. *Maybe,* we thought, *it would be better to get "real" jobs and spin Sojourn out into a bunch of house churches.*

Somewhere along the way, we had what was later referred to as a gospel awakening. The work of Tim Keller in particular gave us a renewed sense of clarity and focus about the purpose of the church and, indirectly, our sense of purpose in ministry. An effort to make clear the dynamics of the gospel—that God is holy, we are sinners, Jesus saves us, and Jesus sends us on mission—became a priority in all our work, and it bore fruit in a church that began to see significant life change and growth at a rate we hadn't imagined. The message being preached, practiced, and sung had a deep resonance for a church that felt like they'd grown up in a church environment where things were emotive but unclear, hospitable but not transformational.

We thought we were brilliant and innovative. "Let's make the gospel the center of everything we do as a church!" Our worship services became cruciform, following the "God is holy, we are sinners; Jesus saves, Jesus sends" dialogue as an architecture for our collective worship and prayer. Of course, all we were doing was reconstructing our shabby, Gen X version of a much larger Christian tradition.

But that sense of discovery (or rediscovery) was palpable for the entire congregation. If you were part of Sojourn, you felt like you were in on a secret. It bred a certain amount of pride, yes, but it also led to a real and dramatic life change. The gospel wasn't an abstraction for people; it was a way of life.

We were renting a facility in the mid-2000s when our growth took off, and we knew we needed a building. We were meeting on Sunday nights still, with as many as six hundred people packed into an out-of-the-way and underequipped church. Word came that an old elementary school was going up for sale a couple of neighborhoods over and that it would have plenty of room to house our church.

The only obstacle was that we were broke. Truly, flat broke.

A donor came forward—someone only loosely connected to the church—and offered to help. The school was being sold at a public auction. If the price wasn't crazy, he'd buy it for us, help us renovate it, and donate it.

I'll never forget that morning. It was just the lead pastor, the donor, another member of the church, and me at the auction, along with the auctioneer and one other bidder. The whole thing took about five minutes. The other guy placed one bid against us, and the building was ours. We spent the next six months raising money and renovating.

It became the 930 Arts Center. On Sundays, it was home to our church gatherings. Throughout the rest of the week, the church offices were on the second floor, but the rest of the building was a vibrant center for the arts. The first floor held a two-thousand-square-foot white-box gallery and two music venues. The second and third floors held office spaces, another gallery, and art studios. At one time it was home to several visual artists and photographers, a graphic design firm, a documentary film company, and a skateboard company. We partnered with local arts organizations and promoters to host people like Yo La Tengo, Bill Frisell, Grizzly Bear, Joe Henry, Shellac, and Over the Rhine.

The church tripled in size over the next few years, and our community of musicians began writing music and collaborating in ways I couldn't have imagined.

I can look back now and see some of the cracks in the veneer. I see the people who didn't make it with us through that season because of burnout or exhaustion. I can see conflicts that I was on the wrong side of. But we were moving so fast—life was moving so fast, with lots of friends getting married and having kids—it was hard to know how seriously to pay attention to any of those cracks. We see what we want to see. We felt invincible. And why wouldn't we?

———X———

Jesus' final week in Jerusalem was provocative. Sometime after arriving in the city, he went to the temple, turning over tables and driving out moneychangers and livestock salesmen (Matthew 21). These moneychangers took whatever money the pilgrims had, be it Roman or Greek or other, and converted it into the acceptable currency of the temple. They would either charge an exorbitant fee for their services or else exact a usurious exchange rate to exploit the foreign pilgrims who had made the long journey to Jerusalem. Notably also, all four of the Gospel writers make specific mention of those in the court selling doves or pigeons (v. 12). These birds were the acceptable sacrifice of the poor who brought no livestock and couldn't afford to buy any at the markets. At every opportunity the poor and vulnerable were being extorted. I find myself less enraged at the predators, though their acts are grievous. I find myself more attuned to their prey.

Imagine yourself as one of these pilgrims, having made a dangerous journey to the city or as an impoverished Jew arriving at the temple. This is the holiest of ground, a place reserved among all the earth where one can draw near to God. But the moneychangers and livestock sellers hold a monopoly on your access to the Lord. If you can't afford to bring your offering with you, or if you can't afford the marked-up price for their doves, you have no way to practice your faith. You are on the wrong side of an enormous amount of power. It must have been a lucrative grift. Pay the price or be left out.

The image of Jesus making a whip of cords is easily misunderstood, the violence crowding out the compassion. Maybe Peter did as much, seeing it through the lens of his dream. Maybe he saw Jesus' actions as a first strike in the war, maybe even echoing Moses' war for the Holy Land or Elijah's war against Canaanite corruption.

We could laugh at Peter dreaming the wrong dream, but we're no different. For as long as I've been a Christian, I've heard the language of war used as a metaphor for ministry. On some level that's to be expected. Jesus does announce the arrival of a kingdom, which has political and military implications, and of course Paul describes the "armor of God" and a war against spiritual darkness. But the church has, from its beginning, fallen into temptation to overextend these ideas, transforming them from spiritual realities and poetic images—language meant to invite our spiritual imaginations into something beyond the power struggles of this world—into a justification of bravado and chest-thumping faux masculinity.

Like Peter, the church has long dreamed of empire. During the centuries of Christendom, this meant land wars throughout Europe and the Middle East, forcing people to kneel before a cross-shaped sword or be killed by it. The leaders of the church and the empire (sometimes the same people) expanded the borders of Christendom, expanding its grasp on people, land, and wealth.

Much of that political vision collapsed after the Reformation and the Enlightenment, though it still resurfaces in modern politics. The rise of Christian nationalism in the United States in recent decades is the clear and present version of those old impulses, but there are other echoes. Consider the ambitions of many churches for ever-larger congregations, buildings, and bank accounts; what is that but hunger for people, land, and wealth?

At Mars Hill Church, Mark Driscoll used to talk about how the expanding church would "own" the city of Seattle as their numbers grew, their members prospered, and they bought land and started businesses. Mars Hill divided ministries between "Air War" (preaching, music, online content) and "Ground War" (small groups, counseling, member care); war metaphors were ubiquitous in Mark's preaching and writing. Staff members saw themselves as soldiers, leaning into the metaphor to justify their sacrifices and the demand for sacrifices by those who served in their ministries.

Mars Hill was hardly alone in this, but they were incredibly influential in their time. The Air War-Ground War concept was adopted by countless churches, including my own.

At times the indulgence in militant metaphor gets absurd, some examples making Mars Hill look tame by comparison (the militant metaphor was central to Kristin Kobes Du Mez's book, *Jesus and John Wayne*). Describing the Stronger Men's Conference in 2020, one speaker celebrated, "You guys, Batman was here, there was hair metal. Bombs went off. There were guns. It was everything you could ever want." The conference also featured bull riding, motocross, MMA, and Mark Driscoll screaming at the audience.

We see what we want to see. And if you want to see Jesus like a cage fighter, wielding a whip and inviting us to take up a sword and go to war, you will. It might be on the battlefield, it might be in a boardroom, it might be on the steps of the Capitol or in a pulpit or a staff meeting: the spirit is the same. We wield this world's power to get power in this world, and if we can turn Jesus' actions in the temple into a justification for violence of our own, we will.

And if that's what we want, at some point the real Jesus will disappoint us. The mob in Jerusalem eventually wearied of his lack of further triumph, and once their patience wore thin, the religious officials saw their opening and had Jesus arrested. Handing him over to the Romans and accusing him of insurrection. When questioned by Pilate, Jesus only made claims on spiritual power rather than political. Still, the mob demanded his execution. In a profoundly revelatory move Pilate offers a choice; I can free Jesus, who says he isn't interested in usurping the governor's authority, or I can free Barabbas—who'd been arrested as part of an uprising (Matthew 27).

Universally, they wanted Barrabas. You can keep your "kingdom come," we want ours now.

It may seem contradictory, what with all the militaristic symbolism, but many evangelicals also love a persecution narrative. Kids in our movement grow up with them, whether they were invited to be Jesus freaks, to indulge fantasies of being martyred for their faith in a school shooting, or to pick fights with professors and tell them "God's not dead." We extend them into our adulthood. Mark Driscoll told Mars Hill Church they existed in a godless city that hated children and had no gospel-preaching churches. Fox News tells Christians their faith is one generation away from being made illegal. Fifteen years ago it was because of the imposition of sharia law. After that, it was because of gay marriage and the war on Christmas. More recently it's been because of immigrants,

Marxism, drag-queen story hour, and "woke" elites (I hate this word, which increasingly is shorthand for "anything I don't like"). Each case is an example of moral panic, more fantasy than reality. But even if we granted that these threats were real, our response to them is still wrong if, when fears arise, we reject the way of Jesus and cry for Barabbas. The persecution narrative merely justifies the militarization of the faith. It turns out that everyone wants to be a martyr, but no one wants to die. We want a revolutionary. We want a fighter. We want a Savior with a sword, not a cross. A pastor with a bully pulpit. A president who will shoot his enemies in the middle of Fifth Avenue.

When I preached on Ephesians 4 in the wake of Trayvon Martin's death, the backlash surprised me. A decade on I think I understand it a little more. When your culture is steeped in fighting for what's yours against relentless threats, it can be easy to forget your neighbor. And in the name of fighting for what's ours, we can make strange bedfellows. We may not be Nazis, but the Nazi next door is fighting for our same cause. The pressures of losing an imagined culture war and facing rejection among our supposed allies mount until it's impossible to bend. Impossible to acknowledge something like racism exists because if you give an inch, you're just certain they'll take a mile and the whole world you were fighting for will come tumbling down. This, I think, is what you would call being stiff-necked. Unwilling to stop telling yourself a story long enough to listen to someone else's.

Jesus indeed sparked a revolution when he cleansed the temple— not spreading outward into the territory beyond but turning inward and reopening all the ways to life with God that had been constrained and inhibited by spiritual and earthly barriers. He drove out the moneychangers and dropped the whip to the floor. What followed was his journey into darkness. A journey he made quietly, testifying to another vision of reality while rejecting worldly power. Soon someone else will pick up a whip, not to join him in the fight but to paint blood-red stripes on his back.

"Take up your cross and follow me," Jesus told his followers. To answer him we must choose which end of the whip we want to be on, to choose between him and Barabbas.

5

Complex Trauma in the Garden of Gethsemane

At the end of the week the disciples gathered for a meal with Jesus. In three years of strange ministry this must have been one of the strangest nights of all.

All week long Jesus talked about judgment, death, resurrection, and eternal life. Tonight was no different. After washing their feet like a servant, he invited his disciples to eat his body and drink his blood, predicted his death again, and proclaimed that one of them would betray him. After dinner, they made their way out of the city, back across the Kidron Valley to a garden in a grove of olive trees that gives the Mount of Olives its name.

Here in Gethsemane the weight of the approaching hour begins to settle on Jesus. He turns to his disciples, reveals his sorrows, and asks them to keep watch over him as he steps away to pray. When he returns, he finds them asleep. He rouses them and asks them again to watch over him, to share his burden. Again, they sleep.

Again, he wakes them, almost begging for them to show they care, to be with him in his grief. But they either can't or won't. After hearing their Teacher talk extensively about his death, you might expect Jesus' level of distress here to spark some awareness that maybe he really does believe he is about to die. But they lie back down, literally indulging their dreams while reality made its way across the Kidron in the form of a small mob of religious leaders, a detachment of Roman soldiers, and a lone betrayer.

When Jesus wakes his disciples for the third time, it is as torchlight flickers through the olive grove. They hear footsteps and clanking armor. As the mob draws closer, the disciples smell the burning oil and pitch of the torches. The accuser enters the grove.

Peter's hand goes to the sword at his hip. Judas greets Jesus with a kiss, identifying him to the authorities before slipping away.

"Who is it you want?" Jesus asks the priests and soldiers.

"Jesus of Nazareth," they say.

"I am he," he says (John 18:4-5), invoking the name of God given to Moses centuries before (see Exodus 3:13-14). The words must have struck them like a hurricane because they fall backward. They stand up and gather themselves and he asks again, repeating his answer, adding, "If you are looking for me, then let these men go."

Peter chafed at Jesus washing his feet. There is no way he will cower away from this fight. This fight is completely of a piece with his dream. He seizes his moment, draws his sword, and swings for the head of the high priest's servant. An earthly tool for an earthly struggle. He doesn't take the head, only an ear (v. 10). Before any more blood can spill, Jesus intervenes, sending Peter backward with a sharp rebuke for the violence. He heals the man's ear and allows himself to be bound and taken away. The torchlight recedes as the mob marches him back across the Kidron, leaving the disciples in a darkness that will haunt them for days to come.

This had to be the moment the spell broke. Peter's hero was being marched off to stand trial. Here in Gethsemane, Peter found himself on the brink of the longest, darkest night of his life. A headlong plunge into the tragic side of life just when he thought the triumph was nearest. He was wholly unprepared for it.

The multisite church was the hot idea in the late 2000s, and it had been on our radar for several years before we decided to try it. I'm convinced it's one of the keys to understanding what went wrong at a lot of our churches.

We used to say that it was a strategy for growth, not a substitute for church planting. If you're in a landlocked neighborhood, or if you want to have parish-style communities where people live where they worship, multisite makes a ton of sense. Rather than spend money on bigger buildings, plant a local campus.

There was an enormous amount of debate about whether these churches should be video venues (with the preacher being broadcast on a screen) or have live local preachers. We chose the latter in part because we were—as always—broke, and the technology to do video well was too expensive.

What I didn't see at the time was the way multisite ministry created a permission structure for truly grandiose ideas. It essentially

blew the cap off any sense of restraint when it came to ambitions
for the church, including how large we could be and what kind of
ministry could develop underneath our umbrella. That became
apparent soon enough. We launched Sojourn East, our first multisite, in 2011, which required whoever was preaching to finish a
sermon at a 9:00 a.m. service downtown, jump in a car to speed
over to the east campus in time to preach for the 10:00 service
there, and then speed back downtown for the 11:00 service back
at midtown.

It was crazily ambitious and utterly exhausting to pull off, especially because you still had to come back and preach two more
services at midtown that night. But it worked. The church grew.
Two more campuses would launch in the next eighteen months.
Fortunately, we managed to recruit preaching pastors to lead all
three of the campuses before long.

But in a way the damage was done. If Sojourn could have an
unlimited number of campuses, what else could we do? How
many churches could we plant around the country? What kind of
educational institutions could we partner with or develop? How
big could our reach and influence get?

I'm not a believer in the idea that unhealthy pastors get themselves into leadership looking for opportunities like this; rather, I
think that the leadership model we have in our evangelical world
incentivizes grandiosity. Maybe that is itself a factor in filtering
who shows up for the job in the first place. But, regardless, there's
a way in which those incentives can bring out the worst in abso-
lutely anybody—including us. I include myself along with other

leaders at my church and our lead pastor. What was going to stop us? What were the limits?

There were many limits, of course, not least of them being the simple limitations of human nature. We were finite, and finitude would catch up with us all.

If there was a tipping point for me, it was the blueberries. It was the summer of 2011 and Sojourn's pastor had recently left for a sabbatical. Before that our executive team (the four of us that led the staff) had navigated three months of an agonizing budgeting process.

Sojourn was a large church by then. We had been launching new campuses since 2010 with weekly attendance growing exponentially, but the church's budget remained strained. When you consider that most new members at any church are slow to adopt giving to the church ministries, that the bulk of our church still comprised young families and singles, and that the largest campus was also in an impoverished neighborhood, you can see why; folks just didn't have a lot of money to give. It made the budget process excruciating. We'd survey each ministry's needs and then spend the next several weeks saying no. We felt like we'd succeeded by leaving every staff member equally unhappy, including the four of us. We would all make sacrifices.

On the first Monday in the office after the pastor left for the sabbatical, there was a small gift for every staff member laid out in neat little rows on the large table in our workroom. They were from him (via his administrative assistant) and had a little note of encouragement about enjoying our summer. We found out the next Monday that it was to be a series. There would be one gift for each week he was gone.

We were exhausted. The sabbatical wasn't just a break for him. It was a break for us. For the next several weeks we could all let our guard down, not having to be ready to react to whatever whirlwind came with him into our next staff meeting. These gifts were, frankly, weekly interruptions of our respite.

There are many great resources out there seeking to understand the common thread between many of the fallen pastors of my generation. These pastors didn't commit sexual or financial sins; they were removed from ministry (or forced to resign) because of concerns about the unhealthy environments they'd created. Every story is different because each leader and each context is different, but I think there are some common threads.

I've been careful here not to get too deeply into the weeds of our story or the details of our team's dysfunction. But from what I experienced at Sojourn and what I've learned in studying other churches in the years since, I think there are two common threads.

The first is the *why* question. It applies especially to the leaders of these communities but also to those, like me, who surround them. Why are you here? What are you after? What is it that is so satisfying about life on a stage or behind a pulpit? What is it offering you?

For almost all of us there's a mixed answer to that. As I said earlier, I don't think anyone shows up in ministry with plans for grandiose kingdom-building, but the world we inhabit cultivates and incentivizes that grandiosity and brings out the worst in us. If you're not clear or not truthful about the why, you may be looking to resolve questions about your life, your soul, or your story from the leader's chair that have nothing to do with "serving the Lord." That lack of awareness is poison.

The second is slightly more involved but best summed up by an episode of *The West Wing*. In it, Josh Lyman has just finished leading a successful presidential campaign for Matt Santos (note: not George Santos). In this episode Josh arrives in DC with the same frenzied, endless energy that he ran with during the campaign. He's yelling at people, throwing things, and generally treating people like garbage. Finally, a mentor pulls him aside to tell him that he's lost his sense of direction. He's not campaigning anymore; he's getting ready to govern, and you can't govern like you campaigned. You'll burn out first.

I think there's something true about this for many of my cohort who entered ministry twenty years ago. We came in feeling like we had to build something from nothing—especially if we were involved in church planting. At no point, though, did it feel like we stopped building. Somehow a church of 500, 1,000, or 3,500 still felt like twelve people in a room, and like it might evaporate overnight if we let our guard down at all.

In truth, trying to live that way doesn't accord with reality. A church of two thousand needs a different kind of leadership from a church of two hundred. Many leaders didn't adjust. Some didn't know how. Some knew how and didn't want to take the necessary steps to do so, fearing the loss of control, loss of meaning, or loss of the *why* discussed earlier. In any case they couldn't shift, and the consequences caught up to them.

Gifts notwithstanding, the hope of getting a break from the chaos evaporated almost instantly. The new budget had required some of us (including me) to tell our teams there would be no raises, that ministry budgets wouldn't grow with the church that year, and that we would have no new hires to fill the gaps that kept us all spread thin. At the time, I was serving as one of our executive pastors, overseeing music, arts, communications, and capital campaigns across the various sites of our church. To their credit the staff all took it well, believing that it was worth sacrificing one more year for the sake of the mission they were a part of.

Around a month later, though, several hires were announced. But the decisions were made without consultation or collaboration with the overall staff team. The results were explosive, and we directed our rage at one another. Some staff members quit. Others followed within a few months. Some members even left the church as word of the conflict and poor treatment spilled out.

It's one of those moments I look back on today with no small amount of regret. Why didn't we call the pastor and say, "Come on back and fix this"? Why did we worry more about settling things down than addressing the rationale behind the hiring decisions?

The harder question for me, though, is why was what I experienced as deception toward the entire staff not enough to make me leave? The answer exposes some hard things for me. On the one hand I was a true believer and every obstacle was seen through the lens of the dream. I held on to a sense of inevitability. Believing everything had to work out in the long run. On the other hand I had my own motivated reasoning for wanting conflicts to resolve neatly. This was my livelihood too. The only real vocation I'd ever had. What would become of my life if the church collapsed?

Tim Smith from Mars Hill Church told me of similar dynamics there. He said, "It always felt like we were one good conversation away from getting it right and making things healthy." As with Peter, these good conversations were the stories we told ourselves to live. The skill of an abusive leader is to maintain an air of possibility with a mixture of charisma, flattery, and performative vulnerability. If you're a true believer in the church's vision, you're biased toward believing that story in the first place. Despite all the warning signs you keep hope alive by telling that story again and again, drowning out reality for as long as you can. This might be the conversation that helps us turn the page.

Such conversations weren't abstractions, either. When the pastor returned from his sabbatical, I arranged for us to meet with an older leader from outside the church, a consultant we'd relied on to help us navigate tensions in the past. I wanted to make his reentry as easy as possible, to break the news of all that had gone on gently enough that it didn't cause an overreaction and more chaos, to prove that I'd handled it for him. I also genuinely wanted to confront the issues and make clear that he needed to change. To my mind that meeting had the tone of an intervention. It wouldn't be the last. About six months later I'd initiate another meeting that was even more confrontational and brought in even more leaders to participate. I'd stage at least two more formal interventions in the next three years and have countless informal conversations on the same problems along the way.

But the truth is the writing was on the wall in the summer of 2011.

Around mid-July, still in the middle of the pastor's sabbatical, the workroom was full of fresh blueberries from a nearby farm. By that time the conflict had gone nuclear, and everybody on staff felt it. I'd thought the gifts were in bad taste from the beginning, but by then I was disgusted. I wasn't alone. A few staff members sampled a handful of the berries here and there, but mostly the fruit sat untouched on the worktable. For days. They began to grow fluffy gray mold while a gelatinous purple ooze ran out of the perforated plastic containers, pooling on the countertop and dripping onto the floor. The pastor's administrative assistant eventually came through to throw them away and clean up the mess. The workroom smelled like rot.

I think back to Hemingway's wry take on going broke. Gradually, then suddenly. That's how my disorientation happened. The dream of starting a church that stays true to its message and its people became a story. It gave me a sense of hope and I would tell myself the story when whiffs of toxic culture would waft through a staff meeting. You keep plausibility kindled like a flame. It may slowly dim, but there's always light. Until one day it suddenly goes out and you find yourself in darkness.

I'd spent years believing that our team was one good conversation away from health, that all the talk of self-awareness, emotional health, and organizational transition was going to bear fruit. I'd had it in my head for a decade or more that this would be the job I'd have for the rest of my career—making music, serving Christian artists, and pastoring a community that felt spiritually homeless. But day by day the evidence piled up that it wasn't going to last. I started having fantasies of finding another job at another church, but when I knocked on those doors, I often found evidence that things weren't much healthier there.

Years later I'd become familiar with a concept known as complex trauma. Trauma as we generally know it happens when nightmares come to life—encounters with death, violence, or sudden loss. Complex trauma is more of a long-term experience, death by a thousand paper cuts. It's the product of years of emotional or spiritual abuse, the kind of thing you see in people who come out of toxic and abusive environments like churches or cults.

Trauma rewires the brain. To dramatically oversimplify it, trauma creates a superhighway between your senses and your lizard brain, the most primitive part of our mind that takes over when threatened and determines whether we'll fight, flee, or try to fawn and flatter the threat to appease it. Posttraumatic stress disorder is the result of the construction of those highways; the traumatized brain lives on high alert and experiences or encounters that are in no way connected to the original trauma nonetheless hit us as danger and light up that superhighway, and we leap into fight-flight-fawn mode. Living on a constant verge takes a tremendous toll on the body and mind.

These changes aren't theoretical; we can map them on MRIs, and it turns out that victims of complex trauma have similar neural malformations as those who experience more sudden trauma.

By 2015 life was on high alert for my wife and me. We both spent Monday nights into Tuesday mornings on the verge of panic, knowing that the regular staff meeting on Tuesday morning could create untold chaos for the week ahead. Neither of us could sleep well. Even in weeks that didn't erupt, I felt like a shell. My counselor, who had been working with many of our staff, began telling me near the first of that year to start planning my exit. Go back to school. Find another church. Maybe find a season away from ministry to decompress and heal.

This was when I began thinking about starting a nonprofit. Build a team, publish newsletters and podcasts, and serve Christians who were trying to think through life in an increasingly secularized world. I worried about many elements of the idea, though. The money. The personnel. The process of leaving. The staff I loved that I'd leave behind.

I also had terrible anxiety about life apart from Sojourn. This is common in unhealthy, idealistic churches. My whole identity was wrapped up in a sense of being part of this place, which also left me anxiously wondering if my ministry could matter at all apart from it. In hindsight I see the absurdity of the fear, but it was all-consuming at the time.

The conflict among the staff had grown increasingly tense. In the past several years our executive team had been in a relentless state of flux. People rotated on and off as they were either let go, marginalized, or burned out and asked to step away. But in the summer of 2015 a new executive pastor stepped in. He truly believed that he and the lead pastor would work together and come up with a plan that brought needed order and left everyone—the staff, the elders, and the church—in a much better situation. You could see it in his eyes. "We're one conversation away."

They talked about the reorganization for much of that summer. By then the word *reorg* itself was a trigger word; we'd been through more of them than we could count. Any one of those structures implemented in a healthy way—specifically, implemented in a way that meant the pastor participated fully in the accountability that was part of the structure—could have brought health. But constant change meant constant instability, which allows a strong-willed personality to triangulate and maintain the only functional authority in the organization.

I left town in November while conversations about transition were midstream. This was my first trip to Israel, where I'd see the landscape in these pages for the first time. I'd been gone two weeks when I landed in Louisville after more than twenty hours on planes and in airports.

As I walked to baggage claim, my phone rang. The conversation was brief. Welcome home. We need you in the office tomorrow;

we're rolling out the new org chart at tomorrow's staff meeting. I asked how that was possible—I hadn't seen it yet. We'll go over it with you; we'll be sure you're good with it. If we need to pivot at the staff meeting we can. Okay, I said. I was exhausted.

I showed up at the office in the morning. The lead pastor and the executive pastor were full of nervous energy. I sensed I was in for bad news. They talked for a few minutes about the approach they'd taken, the decisions they made, the problems this new chart solved for the staff. They kept using the word *decentralize*, which was itself a warning sign to me since I was one of the few central staff, overseeing arts and music at all the campuses.

They finally rolled out a sheet of architectural paper that was large enough to fit the complex structure of our church. We had about thirty-five hundred people at the time and four campuses. At the top was the central staff and executive team, each campus branching out in different directions. I scanned the chart. Scanned it again. My name wasn't on it.

The Sojourn I knew—the story I'd told and the dream I'd held tightly for all those years—had come to an end.

The garden where Jesus prayed was in the heart of an olive tree grove, where the harvested olives were ground by a large stone, their juices filtered and captured in large vessels. With time, gravity would separate the lighter oil from the water, and workers would skim it off the top. The word *Gethsemane* means "oil press."

Today, the site still has an olive grove, with trees that date from as early as the tenth century. A twentieth-century church, the Church of All Nations, sits next to the garden and enshrines a bedrock that is said to be the stone where Jesus prayed.

The giant olive trees are an extraordinary sight. They look as ancient as they are, like a thousand branches that fused into a single organism. Their trunks are wide and gnarled, full of pockmarks and fist-sized empty pits. They communicate agony, beauty, and horror of their own.

I visited Gethsemane on my second trip to the Holy Land. Two years after the org chart. After walking through the garden, I found myself captivated by the trees' world-weariness, their blistered roots that branched out into soil once fertilized by Jesus' blood, sweat, and tears. My wife and I exited the garden and made our way toward the Church of All Nations. Outside, our friend and fellow traveler was waiting, struck by the same world-weariness as I was.

We were deep into a season of darkness. and the heaviness of Gethsemane was stirring much of our own agony. Our friend too was in a season of darkness, weighed by the grief of his losses. We talked for a moment about the garden, the trees, the sense of sorrow and menace they emanated. He brought up the disciples, sleeping nearby, oblivious to the aches in Jesus' soul and the mob that was already descending toward them.

"They weren't ready. Weren't able to stay with him. They didn't know grief yet," he said. "They couldn't. But come here on the other side of trauma . . ." He trailed off for a moment. "You see yourself in those trees."

I thought about the garden's name, about heavy limestone grinding fresh olives, their juices running off the side of the mill and into jars. I'd spent most of my Christian life talking about what it means to be sanctified, and I'd imagined it mostly to be about pious commitments and faithful disciplines. This garden and its long-gone olive press made a better image, though. Life has a tragic, crushing dimension, and there is no dodging it. But it's the crushing, the pouring out of ourselves that refines us. In time we may settle, and the sanctified oil can be skimmed.

I looked back through the iron bars and into the olive grove. I could see myself lying beside the disciples and lost in a dream of my own. But I could also see myself feeling alone on a dark night, weeping under the shelter of the old tree's branches.

"He was alone," my friend said. "We were never alone. That's what this place means."

6

Golgotha and the Silence of God

Jesus was marched back across the Kidron Valley to the home of the high priest on the eastern slope of Mount Zion. He was likely taken to the basement, where he was beaten by guards while religious leaders debated his fate upstairs.

Today, there's a church on the site known as the Church of Saint Peter in Gallicantu. Like the Church for All Nations, it's modern, built in the 1930s, but constructed atop the ruins of Byzantine and Crusader-era churches. Christians have been worshiping and praying here for a long time.

I felt like I was standing on the set of a golden-age film when we walked through it. The white exterior dazzles in the sun, and the sanctuary is a technicolor array of painted columns, frescos, and mosaics.

The courtyard looks out over the Kidron Valley, lined with stone columns and arches. A statue was built around one of them, depicting a seated man in the middle of an argument with a young woman, a boy, and a Roman soldier. On the roof of the church is a black cross with a golden rooster perched on top.

Of all the places I've visited in the Holy Land, this is one of the least crowded. I wonder if it's because we are deeply uncomfortable with what events that took place here.

While Jesus sweated out a long night in chains below the buildings that once stood here, Peter waited outside in the courtyard, where officials and servants of the high priest had built a fire. He stood at the edge of the firelight, trying to keep his face in the shadows. Eventually, a young woman recognized him and accused him of being one of Jesus' disciples.

"I don't know him," he said (Luke 22:57).

Peter's denial was a favorite subject of motivational talks when I was a kid. Youth pastors featured it in sermons that also described in detail how, at any moment, masked gunmen might burst through the door and demand that we renounce our faith or die. These situations happened all the time, they said, all over the world, and when the tribulation begins or the New World Order takes over, they'd happen here too. Would you be like Peter, or would you be like one of the church's great martyrs and refuse to renounce Jesus?

This subject took on new potency after the mass shooting at Columbine High School in 1999 when the stories of Cassie Bernall and Rachel Scott brought this scenario to life. Cassie was a seventeen-year-old student killed in the massacre. In the days after the shooting the story spread that moments before she was shot, her killer asked if she believed in God, and she said yes.

Later reporting revealed the story to be false, but that didn't deter the Christian subculture's momentum in lionizing Bernall. Christian contemporary music star Michael W. Smith wrote a song titled "This Is Your Time" celebrating Bernall. It won Dove Awards for song and music video of the year. A movie celebrating the martyr narrative of Scott was released as recently as 2016.

In an article in *Vox* called "After Columbine, Martyrdom Became a Powerful Fantasy for Christian Teenagers," Alissa Wilkinson reported the immediate effect of these stories on Christian teenagers. (I'm indebted to that article for much of the information in this section.) Wilkinson writes, "They prompted not just teenage soul searching but also that other teenage phenomenon: aspiration. [Hanna] Rosin described a 'kind of teenage hysteria, a Christian-sanctified death wish' that the Columbine martyrdom mythology had inspired."

A teenager named Tina Leonard, Rosin reported, told a Southern Baptist news service that "God has laid it on my heart that I'm going to be martyred. When I told one of my friends, he said, 'That's awesome. I wish it could happen to me.'"

That might sound horrifying. But for many Christian teenagers in the late 1990s and early 2000s, it made a strange kind of sense. If you were a Christian teenager during the time following the era of the grunge-and-flannel dropout Gen Xers, following your faith was preached to you as a radical act. *Extreme* and *radical* and *fully sold out* were common terms in Sunday school curriculums, at youth rallies, and in teen-focused devotionals and study Bibles.

The rhetoric of radical faith had been around for a while, growing out of the Jesus People movement of the 1970s and reinvigorated through the Christian subculture in 1995, when Christian artists DC Talk released an album titled *Jesus Freak*. It sold more than half a million copies in its first month and has sold more than two million in the two decades since.

Of course, the lionization of martyrs is nothing new. The emperor Constantine deliberately sought to highlight the stories of martyrs, and the feast days of the church calendar feature them prominently. Two of the most important books in church history are collections of martyrs' stories: *The Golden Legend*, published in 1481, and *Foxe's Book of Martyrs*, published in 1563.

It's no wonder, then, that Bernall's story would take root so quickly and powerfully after Columbine. It takes nothing away from the horror of her death or the sincerity of her faith to reexamine this narrative, especially when you consider the knock-on effect of how they're framed. The stories we tell shape our moral imaginations; if we only talk about moments of life-and-death crisis as opportunities for profound courage, we don't provide a category for other kinds of crises. Not everyone can face suffering with unflinching courage. Peter's story shows how God gives us grace nonetheless.

To put it a little differently, the stories of martyrs echo the story of Stephen, the church's first martyr from the book of Acts. Peter's denial belongs in the same conversation, but there is an element of weakness in it. In that way Peter's story can be an emblem for all of us who have failed in our courage in big and small ways. Jesus wasn't done with Peter, and he isn't done with us.

The night of Jesus' crucifixion must have been an extraordinary experience of trauma for the disciples who stayed close enough to witness it. In the Bible it seems like nine of the disciples—all but Peter, John, and Judas—went into hiding. Judas chased his shame into the field of blood where he took his own life. John and Peter followed Jesus to Caiaphas's house, and we know for certain that John followed him all the way to the crucifixion. We also know that at some point several women joined John and witnessed these events, including Jesus' mother, Mary. For these men and women it was the darkest night of the soul imaginable. Every chant of the crowd, every striking fist, every lash of the whip was an eruption of violence against their hopes and dreams. The disillusionment that took place between Jesus' arrest and his resurrection was short—three days—but what it lacked in duration it made up in brutal intensity.

For those of us who've experienced our spiritual traumas, it's often the opposite. Our stories often fit the category of *complex trauma*, which makes up for what it lacks in intensity with relentlessness. It usually begins in ways we may not even notice, and often it simmers in ways that leave us uncertain of our thoughts and emotions. *Am I crazy? Is this really happening? Am I alone in feeling like something is wrong?* It can take years to permit ourselves to acknowledge that indeed something was wrong and to unravel the ways it warped our thinking, our emotions, and our relationships.

I've struggled to know which of my own stories to share here. As I said at the beginning of this book, the characters that surrounded me aren't public figures, and yet my story is a real encounter with loss and grief. So, with that caveat, I'll offer a window into those experiences, attempting to walk a tightrope as I do so.

The days after I met with the pastors who org-charted me out of my role at the church were a roller coaster. Initially, I felt some optimism if you can believe that. That probably speaks to how deep into dysfunction I was. My subconscious didn't even respond to the flagrant unprofessionalism of the whole charade. It just saw the way out.

I planned to start a nonprofit, creating content for Christians thinking about the challenges of living in a world that was often hostile to their faith. This was 2015, and the cultural currents were radically different than they are today. Those of the political left had the bully pulpit at the time. Bakers and florists were getting sued because of their conscientious objections to serving same-sex weddings. The federal government was suing nuns who didn't want to pay for birth control. Donald Trump had announced his run for the presidency, but few people were taking it seriously. He was a reality-TV-show host. Friends of mine who were deeply tied to Republican politics saw Trump's candidacy as a flash in the pan. "It's going to be [Marco] Rubio," one said, again and again. The political establishment would keep rolling on as scheduled.

A commitment to cover my salary for a season provided a generous runway to get the nonprofit started. Along with that were effusive promises to support the work, help raise funds, and ensure that it succeeded. I was also told that there was a desire for me to continue to mentor some of the worship leaders who had come up through my teams over the years. It felt like I was going to still be part of the fabric of the church, and I'd still be connected to aspects of ministry that I valued most. This just might be an evolution that turns out healthy for me.

A couple of weeks later, though, at the end of an executive team meeting, I asked what the timeline was for my exit from that team. It was November and my official transition wasn't until January.

"Oh, yeah," the pastor said. "You're out. You're done." I looked around the room at the other surprised faces on the team. The curtain lifted for me. These last conversations weren't leading to health. They were just words. The truth was I had been eliminated in whatever category of obstacle I had become.

"Okay," I said, trying to hide my surprise at the response. "See ya, suckers," I joked.

I gathered my things and started to walk toward the door, turning around to ask, "Do we want to talk about my involvement with the other worship leaders? Or the other transitions?"

"Yeah, we'll figure that out."

We never figured it out.

A couple of weeks later, at a membership meeting, my exit from the church after fifteen years was announced in a matter of about twenty seconds.

A couple of months later, during a sermon, the pastor was teaching on gratitude. He was preaching effusively about how much the church's arts ministry had improved in recent months. "I'm more proud of our music now than I've been in the last ten years." That phrase hit me pretty hard, almost like an erasure.

These details barely scratch the surface of the disorientation of that year. The fallout of my leaving Sojourn impacted some of my family's closest friendships. Sarah and I were suddenly disconnected. Even though being on staff had become untenable, it was still a tectonic shift. I would eventually come to understand the true breadth and depth of the loss, but at the time the main feeling was isolation. Even just not going into the office and seeing the same people every day was a big change. So many close relationships started to drift.

That was just the private side of things, though. While we were feeling that growing disconnect from our longtime community, we watched the elder statesmen of our evangelical community line up to support a candidate for president whose public and private conduct violated almost everything we'd been taught by those same leaders. Revered theologians were suddenly arguing the biblical case for border walls. Even after the infamous *Access Hollywood* tape, where Trump boasted to the show's host that he could get away with anything—including grabbing women "by the p____"—because he was famous, evangelical leaders lined up, one after another, to dismiss it as "locker room talk" or calling him a "baby Christian" who hadn't known better at the time.

I continued to write and speak based on the values I'd held for years, for instance no political gain is worth turning our backs on the kind of life Jesus calls us to. No strong man is worth staining the public witness of the church. I believed that I surely spoke for a silent majority on these questions. Friends and family pulled me aside to ask why I was sanctioning the murder of babies. My Twitter mentions filled up with neo-Nazis suggesting I be tossed in an oven or Christians spouting psychotic conspiracy theories, calling me a liberal, and all manner of other insults. One notorious Christian news-and-culture website featured a photo of me on their front page with the caption "We'd take him seriously if he didn't look like a fat lesbian." It turns out the majority was not very silent.

Trump won the election at the beginning of November 2016. At the end of the same month a leader at Sojourn submitted a formal complaint against the lead pastor and initiated an account-ability review process that hadn't been in place during my tenure. The issues were the same as those that I'd raised for many years behind the scenes. It was now going to play out in view of the whole church. The pastor was put on a leave of absence while the basis of the complaint underwent investigation. What had been a simmering, almost numbing pain for me—a pain more of absence than presence—suddenly sharpened into a blade, violently severing connections to friends that went back ten, fifteen, even twenty years. Because people would ask me what I thought, and I would tell them what they hoped not to hear.

The pastor's leave of absence extended into 2017, and numerous elders, counselors, and other advisers made efforts to reconcile and heal the broken relationships among the leaders. The staff described a culture of burnout and exhaustion. This validated my sense of weariness. Maybe the voice in my head saying *something isn't right* was telling the truth. Most of these conversations had happened innumerable times before. The process, though, didn't bring feelings of resolution. In many ways it only intensified my disorientation. How much of my life have I given to this? What have we lost? How has this affected—how will it affect—my marriage, our children?

In March 2017 I had a single conversation with Sojourn's lead pastor during that process. He had been meeting with a counselor to work on self-awareness, guiding him toward a reconciliation process. As the conversation started, like so many times before, I felt that gut-level hope: We're one conversation away—is this it?

It wasn't.

I'm not sure it would serve anyone to relitigate the conflict here. Things were simply too far gone. We saw the church, one another, and the stories of our lives differently, and there was no apparent way to bridge the gap. We lived in different worlds.

That was the last time the pastor and I spoke. He resigned a few weeks later, and things got strangely quiet and deeply lonely for Sarah and me again.

I looked back at the seventeen years leading up to that season. We had such a profound sense of community and purpose that guided us. It felt like it would last forever. "I hope I do this until

I retire," I'd say. It felt like we'd found something magical that would last forever. Can't we just stay here?

But slowly, then all at once, the spell had broken. I felt a tiredness and brokenness that I cannot, even years later, put into words.

Earlier that night, while they were eating the Passover dinner together, Jesus had warned the disciples that they would scatter after his arrest. "But I'll meet you in Galilee," he said.

Peter objected just as he had objected to Jesus saying he would go to Jerusalem, suffer, and die, just as he had objected to Jesus washing his feet. It was the objection born of not hearing the story Jesus was telling him, instead, Peter was listening to the story he was telling himself. "I will never fall away," he said.

Jesus knew what the night held for Peter and told him. "Before the rooster crows today, you will deny three times that you know me" (Luke 22:34).

I see myself in Peter at that moment. The assurance that the dream won't end, the certainty, the come-what-may confidence. It's the same spirit that makes the stories of martyrs so appealing, that makes us want to amplify and intensify them. The courage of Jesus facing death might feel out of reach for many of us. I know it does to me. But when we see heroes like Stephen or the list of names in *Foxe's Book of Martyrs*, we think, *That could be me*. We, like Peter, want to imagine that should the crisis come, we'd stand strong.

———X———

Outside Caiaphas's house, firelight flashed across Peter's face, catching the eye of one of the high priest's servants. She accused Peter of having been one of Jesus' disciples. "I don't know what you're talking about," he said. Later, another accused him of the same. "I don't know the man." Then a third accusation. This time, accompanied by curses, he says again: "I do not know the man" (Matthew 26:74).

What are we seeing? Are we seeing a coward afraid of being tossed in the dungeon alongside Jesus? Are these simply the words of a liar? I'm not sure.

Don't get me wrong, Peter is obviously lying. But the thing about language is that it often communicates more than one thing at a time. In this case, while telling the woman "I don't know what you're talking about" is an evasive lie, his other statement is intriguing: "I don't know the man."

There's a way in which he's telling the truth. Underneath the surface lie is the most disturbing reality of Peter's life. Jesus, this modern-day Elijah who would liberate Israel and restore it to its unique glory among the nations of the world, was on a death march. Peter couldn't recognize him. Was he a fraud?

At some level Peter had spent his years with Jesus seeing what he wanted to see. It didn't matter how many times Jesus had predicted his death, Peter still read all the signs in a way that fits the mold of his dream. And he wasn't a coward. Earlier that night he'd drawn his sword, ready for battle. Hours later, standing in that courtyard, he wasn't ready for a fight, and I think in part it was because he didn't know what he would be fighting for. This was not the revolution he expected. But Jesus told him to put the weapon away. It wasn't a time for victory; it was a time for losing. Jesus was walking toward unimaginable suffering, and he knew Peter wasn't ready to go with him. "But I'll meet you in Galilee," he said, offering a cryptic spark of hope.

The scene outside Caiaphas's house that night, where Peter denies knowing Jesus, is both a lie and a truth. On an empirical level, of course, he knows Jesus. On a deeper level he doesn't know this Jesus at all. A complicated denial.

They say that denial is the first stage of grief, and I know that was true for me. Believing that we were one step away from making things right at the church required a heavy dose of denial. In the years that followed the pastor's departure, as we watched Sojourn change and transition, at times feeling alien to us, I still lived in denial. I believed that if I got involved in the right ways or if leaders made a few changes, we could get back to the magic of the community we'd fallen in love with two decades before. I didn't want to allow myself to think there was no going back.

That's why I have a much deeper compassion for Peter as he stood outside Caiaphas's house. He wasn't afraid of his own death; he was afraid of the death of his dream.

After his third denial, a rooster crowed. Reality crashes in on Peter. He had scattered. The same Jesus he'd loved and had pledged to follow to the end had known all along that he wouldn't. John tells us that Jesus caught Peter's eye at that moment, indicating that he'd either not been taken into the chambers below Caiaphas's house or he was already being moved. Matthew and Mark describe Peter walking outside the courtyard and weeping bitterly.

Some scholars suppose that Peter may have witnessed the crucifixion, though no direct mention of that exists in the Scriptures. This conjecture is based on a passage in the Gospel of Luke that says, "all those who knew him . . . stood at a distance watching these things" (Luke 23:49), and some suppose that Peter would have stayed with or near John, who we know from his Gospel was at Golgotha.

Whatever the case, it was a long, dark night and a long, dark day that passed before Jesus' death. Whether Peter wandered off alone or in search of other disciples, or if he stood at a distance and watched Jesus die, there's no doubt that Golgotha was an unforgettable milestone. This hill, just outside the old city walls, was a familiar place of torture and execution. After his death, Jesus' body was taken to a nearby tomb so it could be quickly and properly buried before the Sabbath began. Night fell, and the silence of God fell with it as the disciples regathered, full of anxiety and fear. It was Peter's first night without the dream.

7

Whispers at Mount Sinai

Let's go back to Mount Tabor for a moment. Back to the blinding light of Jesus' glory, to the stunning presence of Elijah and Moses, to the weight of that moment and what it meant in the mind and heart of Peter, and what it confirmed about the dream that had taken up residence in his heart and his spiritual imagination. The brilliance of this dream, how incredibly close it felt on Mount Tabor, creates the unbearable cognitive dissonance with the reality of Jesus, arrested, mocked, beaten, scorned, flayed, and executed. Dead in a tomb.

These visions didn't fit together; the bleach-white light of the transfiguration, the ashen linen that now wrapped Jesus' dead body, and the stony blackness of the tomb as the stone rolled shut against it. Peter had expected Elijah: fire from heaven, a land cleansed of evil. What he'd gotten instead . . . I don't think he had a name for it. "I don't know him."

But maybe Peter didn't know Elijah either.

There's a scene in Mel Brooks's film *Blazing Saddles* that has come to mean a great deal to me in recent years. Cowritten by Richard

Pryor (among others), the movie itself is a scandalous and un-flinching send-up of the racism that was baked into American culture at the time. Bart, the film's lead, was a Black railroad worker sentenced to death after hitting his boss over the head with a shovel. (The boss had left him for dead in quicksand moments before.) Rather than being sent to the gallows, he was sent to Rock Ridge to be the new sheriff—an attempt to drive the town's citizens out. When he arrives, their shock that the governor sent them a Black sheriff turns to anger, and Bart narrowly escapes a lynching before retreating into the sheriff's office.

But he isn't deterred. "Once you establish yourself, they have to accept you," he tells his friend. In the next scene he greets an old woman on the sidewalk as she passes by. She responds by calling him the N-word. Cut to the interior of the sheriff's office moments later, where his friend asks him, "What did you expect? Welcome, sonny? Make yourself at home? Marry my daughter? You've got to remember that these are just simple farmers. These are people of the land. The common clay of the new West. You know . . . morons." Like most of the movie, there's a profound truth beneath the joke. Sometimes our expectations are the source of our pain.

Peter looked at Elijah and saw a conquering hero. But he was only paying attention to part of the story.

When Elijah humiliated the prophets of Baal, the crowd of on-lookers fell to the ground and cried out, "The LORD—he is God!"

(1 Kings 18:39). They then slaughtered the prophets, cleansing the land of their oppression. Elijah then prayed for rain, and it came. Ahab fled to Jezreel, unable to deny what he'd seen with his own eyes. Mission accomplished.

And yet it wasn't. Jezebel responded to all Ahab told her by promising to kill Elijah, and the menace of humiliation and death overwhelmed him. He fled to the desert, collapsed under a broom tree, and prayed for death. "I've had enough," he said. "Take my life; I am no better than my ancestors" (1 Kings 19:4). I give up. I turned and ran. I failed. And I wish I were dead. It's the cry of disillusionment and despair.

The broom tree (sometimes called the juniper) grows in arid places, drawing water from deep beneath the surface from long and extensive root systems, growing wide branches that produce small white flowers. They're highly adaptable, each one growing to suit the environment. Some are broad and flat like an umbrella. Others are scrubby and thin, and sometimes, when exposed to the wind, they're sculpted into exotic arcs. When the juniper tree is especially dry, it sheds flowers, leaves, and branches, making a bed of needles and fine twigs beneath it. The dried roots, while toxic, were a valuable commodity because of their ability to burn hot for a long time.

As a symbol the broom tree appears throughout the Scriptures. Its poisonous roots were the food of mockers (Job 30) and were ignited to make the coals that burned liars (Psalm 120). It's broom-like branches were used to build the tabernacle and tents of the Israelites as they traveled through the desert and to sweep them clean. Some interpreters identify it as the tree where Hagar laid Ishmael when she feared abandonment by God, and some believe the burning bush itself was a broom tree. Throughout the Prophets, it appears as a sign of renewal after suffering.

Taken together, we see two ideas. The first is *purification*: it's the broom that sweeps, the coals that purge, the poison that silences lies. The second is *encounter*, and not just any encounter; it's the destination for the lost, the weary, and those that feel like God has abandoned them.

Let's fast forward to a year or two after I'd left full-time ministry at the church. About a year later, an investigation began into our lead pastor's dysfunctional patterns of leadership. When the charges were affirmed, a restoration process began. That process failed and he resigned, acknowledging failure of leadership in his letter.

There's much I could say about this season. In many ways it was a critical crossroads for my wife and me, affirming that we were indeed not crazy; things had been bad, the demands had been unreasonable, and ministry wasn't supposed to look this way. But it also left us rattled. Many of our friendships were ripped apart. Some still aren't restored.

At the same time that this was happening, Trumpism continued to rise and make life difficult for those of us who'd spoken against his nomination and election in 2016. The nonprofit venture I'd begun after leaving the church got shelved, and I started a small business producing media for churches, nonprofits, and anyone willing to hire us and keep our lights on.

I collapsed under my own sort of broom tree in 2017. It's difficult to convey the weight that converged in my heart with the spreading stain of Trumpism on the broader church and the spreading division and fallout in the church I had helped launch and that had felt so much like a long-lost home. Having the truth come to light was affirming, but my life felt derailed and kept derailing.

The ministry I'd founded and led after leaving Sojourn was transforming day by day as the culture I was hoping to engage boiled and mutated, which wasn't necessarily a bad thing, but it also wasn't what I'd signed up for as a leader. I watched friend after friend grow disillusioned with the church and step away from it. Marriages failed. Pastors and leaders I mentored—seemingly one after another—had moral failures or lost faith (or both) and left the ministry.

I watched friends—pastors of other churches I'd grown alongside—struggle as I watched their churches implode in conflict. I also watched a broader church that seemed either blissfully unaware or content to ignore the emerging patterns. Pastors like Mark Driscoll who'd fallen and left the ministry started new churches and whitewashed their pasts. Others started leadership consulting businesses, proving once and for all that irony was dead.

Many prominent churches chose to pander to the new political realities, and Christian nationalism went from being a fringe idea to something accepted and normalized in the mainstream. My friend Russell Moore was leading the Ethics and Religious Liberty Commission of the Southern Baptist Convention. This organization was essentially the public policy and political engagement wing of the SBC, advocating for issues like the protection of religious freedom in the United States and overseas or for the pro-life cause. Issues like immigration, race in the United States, and Trumpism had already created tensions for Russell in the SBC. He had gone public in defense of ideas that, again, I thought were more than supported by the full testimony of Scripture. Such ideas were branded as liberal by many others in the convention. But when Russell began to surface and highlight problems with sexual abuse in the SBC in 2018, I saw a groundswell rise against him—something I don't think I'll ever understand.

In the years that followed, survivor advocates like Moore and Rachael Denhollander—the whistleblower in the USA Gymnastics sexual-abuse scandal and an attorney and advocate herself—were branded enemies of the church. Somehow sexual abuse became a kind of partisan issue, and the dividing lines happened to match those that separated Trump supporters and never-Trumpers in the SBC. (That doesn't seem coincidental, given the allegations surrounding Donald Trump.)

I found myself wondering—like so many people I knew—what was even real anymore. I'd given my entire adult life to launching and helping lead a church, and I'd become disconnected from it so suddenly I hardly had a moment to acknowledge or react to it. Our "friends are friends forever" community was suddenly brittle.

Meanwhile, highly visible leaders in the large church I'd grown up respecting became bootlicking pundits, contorting both their spines and the Scriptures to provide apologetics to support their naked embrace of power politics. Both near and far I had lost my sense of spiritual belonging.

Going to church was agonizing. For the first time in my life the last thing on earth I wanted to hear was worship music. Getting ready on Sundays felt like wading through mud and sludge, everything in me resisted showing up. When I was there, my skin was on fire and the entire service felt like a confrontation with what I'd lost: friends, community, intimacy with God, music, and music-making. Sometimes I'd barely be able to sit through it, taking long, strolling walks around the building, hoping not to bump into anyone, slipping in just in time to show up at the Communion table and grasp the bread and wine as something concrete that, I prayed, would reconnect me with Christ and maybe even the body. But there was an awful silence.

Surrounded by a bone-white desert and crying out for death, Elijah fell asleep. Amid the kind of soul-weariness Elijah was experiencing, I'm sometimes surprised he could fall asleep. But I think it was the first of several signs of grace.

The second came when he awoke. An angel stood over him, inviting him to rise and eat. Elijah turned his head to find bread and water next to him. He ate and drank, lying down to sleep again. The angel woke him again a while later. "Get up and eat

some more, or the journey ahead will be too much for you"
(1 Kings 19:7 NLT). So he did.

There's more than a hint of the miraculous in this moment. I
think for most of my life I saw it in the presence of the angel and
maybe—like the loaves and fishes—the miraculous provision of
food. Today, I see it far more in the kindness of God.

In a spiritual framework that idealizes martyrdom, fetishizes
persecution, and tries to turn every hardship and obstacle into evidence of spiritual oppression, Elijah's exhaustion should be dis-
comfiting, to say the least. The prophet, by many standards, lost
his way. Sure, there are people out to kill him, but he's faced death
before. Imagine what the prophets of Baal would have done to
him if he'd failed on Mount Carmel. The natural response for
someone who's at a remove from Elijah is to be mystified by his
hopelessness. How can Jezebel's threat have this much menace for
him? Hasn't God demonstrated that he'll do what needs to be
done? These are questions asked only from the cheap seats. I don't
know many people who have been through a journey like this (or
a journey like mine) who are quick to sign on for criticism and
condemnation of the weary prophet.

Elijah is still a prophet here, still revealing something about God
and humanity. In this case it's not a vision of God's grandiosity but
of human finitude. Elijah wants to die because the strength of will
and the resources of courage and bravery had been tapped dry.
Think back to Bart, the sheriff in *Blazing Saddles*. He thought some
genteel kindness would win people over from their racist hatred of
him. The harsh confrontation with his wrongness sent him reeling.

Elijah thought surely the display on Carmel would end the rejection of God and he could finally rest. Rebuked with such venom, something in him just gave out. Like soldiers who've been on a battlefield for months on end, he'd found his breaking point.

But note what doesn't happen; God doesn't demand more from Elijah—at least not yet. He doesn't present Elijah with ideas and visions, doesn't overwhelm him with his presence, and doesn't scold him for losing faith. Instead, he meets him at the most basic and primitive level. He meets him in his body. He provides a broom tree with a bed of drying leaves and flowers. He gives him the gift of sleep, wakes him to feed him, and lets him sleep again. When he wakes the second time, he feeds him again to strengthen him for the long journey ahead.

Richard Foster once said that the most sanctifying thing some people can do is take a nap. The psalmist says God gives sleep to those he loves. Recent work on the science of sleep and the effects of complex trauma confirms that there are physical and neurological effects that follow from spiritual abuse and disorientation. The effect on the body is such that they act like kind of a roadblock. You won't get anywhere in dealing with the soul until you've cared for the body, given it time to catch up, and come to grips with what you've experienced. We live on edge for years, maybe decades, and until the fire that's burning in our minds cools—something that only happens with a certain amount of rest and time—we can't even begin to address other kinds of healing.

So, Elijah eats and drinks again and sets off to meet God again at Mount Sinai.

The mercy of God on display with Elijah is an example of how we might step back from judgment when we encounter people on their journeys of spiritual recovery. There's an impulse in most of us to respond to someone's weariness and despair with prescriptions—pray this, study that, confront that person. In reality none of those can even happen, not in any life-giving way, until the fires burning inside the body have cooled long enough to even assess the wounds.

Healing might take years. There's simply no rushing it, and there ought not to be. God will address Elijah's despair. Hunger and weariness aren't a distraction from healing; they are where healing begins. God knows how he made us. He knows no matter how hard we look for the fences that separate body, mind, and soul, we won't find them. And so God begins caring for Elijah's despair at the most basic and concrete place: his body.

Mount Sinai sits (appropriately enough) on the Sinai Peninsula, a triangle of land that extends south of Israel. On the eastern edge of the peninsula is the Gulf of Aqaba and beyond it, Saudi Arabia and the Asian continent. The Gulf of Suez forms the western edge, and Africa beyond that. To the north are the Mediterranean Sea and Europe. It looks like a wide, blunt blade that's been stabbed into the Red Sea, the crossroads of continents, religions, and histories that are the foundations of Western history. Joseph crossed the Sinai Peninsula on his way to captivity in Egypt. Moses and the Israelites fled their chains across the same peninsula centuries later. Another Joseph led his wife and child back across it again to avoid Herod's call for the death of Bethlehem's sons. Jesus returned later, called out of Egypt and back to Jerusalem to face his destiny. At nearly 7,500 feet, Mount Sinai is the highest peak of those mentioned in this book. The mountain range it's part of is geologically very different too, made up of red and brown volcanic granite that erupts out of canyons in spectacular, striated layers. One can imagine the bone-white wilderness of southern Judea giving way to this bloodier, equally forbidding landscape as Elijah journeyed on foot.

His journey from the broom tree to Sinai took forty days and forty nights—the same length of time Goliath taunted the armies of Israel, the great flood covered every living thing on earth, and later Jesus fasted in the wilderness. Like the broom tree, this length of time is a loaded symbol, reminding us that Elijah's long-suffering wasn't without purpose. There's an intersection with God at the other end of forty days and forty nights, and Elijah would soon have his.

At Sinai he makes his way to a cave and sleeps again. God wakes him by asking, "What are you doing here, Elijah?"

Elijah replies, "I have been very zealous for the LORD God Almighty. The Israelites have rejected your covenant, torn down your altars, and put your prophets to death with the sword. I am the only one left, and now they are trying to kill me too" (1 Kings 19:9-10).

Notice the layers of disillusionment. He's zealous—another true believer—and yet the circumstances have left him asking what

LAND OF MY SOJOURN

the point was. "They" have broken their vows—proven to be hypocrites—and killed the other prophets. Put differently, Elijah is saying, "They've all proven to be liars, and the ones that aren't liars have been crushed by the rest."

Tearing down the altars is a powerful image as well. At the surface we see an act of profane vandalism, destroying an artifact that is the heart and height of their religious practice. That's bad enough, but there's something more subtle here too. These altars aren't just objects; they're places. Meaningful because they're meaning-filled. Our sacred spaces are sacred because of the stories that happened there. Yes, God shows up at Israel's altars and temples, but he doesn't show up in the abstract; he shows up in the particular lives of particular people. It's not hard to imagine an old married couple making the trip to the altar. Maybe they bickered on the entire road to Jerusalem because the ground was hot or because she brought the wrong food or he brought the wrong blankets, but beneath it, really, they argued because their son had stopped speaking to them weeks before. This couple came to the altar wondering if they'd see their grandson, see if the divine presence might work some grace they dare not pray for. Or see a boy leading a lamb through the temple gates, his parents watching him knowing that at seven or eight years old, this will probably be the first worship experience that will stay in his memory for the rest of his life. Or see an old woman carrying a dove, not sure what time she has left, her face marked by the weight of long life but her eyes alight in anticipation of the songs, the dancing, the smells of the feast, the energy of the crowd, and the children.

See your own holy places. The building where you walked an aisle and promised to love someone forever. The place you were baptized or took your First Communion. The place where people gathered around you, laid on hands, and prayed for you as you became a pastor or a deacon or joined a church staff. The place where music and Scripture made you feel like your heart might just lift right out of your chest. The church that felt like home and you thought would last forever, a place that seemed to promise you'd never be lonely again.

Of course, this kind of place isn't confined to a building. The place I lost exists in a series of images and sounds, most of which are both sacred and haunted. There's a night under the stars after a wedding, my not-quite-three-year-old daughter dancing to bluegrass with little LED votive candles clutched in her hands like treasures. This memory remains sacred for me but also full of pain in the background. I can see the faces of friends who left the church because of the toxic culture. I see others who left because our church became too woke. One is gone because of moral failure. Another is because of QAnon-like conspiracies driving wedges between him and everyone. There are countless other nights gathered around kitchen tables, full of laughter and stories and tears.

And then there's music. More than anything or anywhere else, music was the place for me. It was the place where, growing up, I sensed the possibility of deep spiritual community, even though I was the teenage outsider looking in. At Sojourn I experienced it for myself.

There's a thing that happens when musicians play together that's hard to describe if you haven't experienced it. There's probably an analog in sports, when you see a no-look pass and a dunk on a fast break or when a pressured quarterback makes a blind throw knowing his receiver will get to the ball. There's also probably one in acting, a feeling that everyone is telling the same story in the same rhythm. In music it's almost an out-of-body experience. Everyone is in sync and the stage transforms. You're no longer playing the song; you're riding the current. Playing without thought. You sense three or four steps ahead what everyone else is going to do. But it's all unconscious, happening almost without noticing it. But you do notice it, and you try to ride the edge of knowing and not knowing it's happening because if you get caught thinking about it, it disappears.

This is an experience available to artists and others whether they're part of a church or not. Perhaps my favorite common grace. I shared it with a dozen people with whom I'd shared so many important and foundational life experiences. And the music we made was purposeful, rich with the language and stories of life, death, God, the devil, salvation, resurrection, hope, and grief. Experiencing musical communion along with deep spiritual communion Sunday after Sunday, year after year.

Bach supposedly wrote SDG at the top of each composition he wrote for the church. It was shorthand for *Soli Deo Gloria*, "to God alone be the glory." We were far more influenced by Tom Petty and Pearl Jam than Bach, but I think something of that ethic was alive in us. Music was this thing we, our church, and God loved. And for a long time, it was a blessed thing.

Not every Sunday felt that way. Plenty were musical disasters too. But some moments were—and are—indescribably sacred. I remember Sundays when something beautiful happened at the morning services, and people were so moved that the normally sparse evening services were standing-room only. I remember an Easter Sunday when we played Don Francisco's "He's Alive," a Dolly Parton staple of gospel homecomings when I was a kid. People thought it was a joke when I suggested it, and yet when we hit the closing choruses and Meg Schaeffer began singing "He's alive and I'm forgiven, heaven's gates are open wide," the whole church exploded with shouts and tears of joy.

One sacred moment happened on (of all places) a public radio show on the local NPR affiliate, where we were invited to sing a few of our original songs and some old hymns. The broadcast ended with a few hundred strangers singing "It Is Well with My Soul" in perfect harmony.

Another happened miles from home, at the White Arc Studios in Bloomington, Indiana. It was nearly midnight, and we were gathered around an old piano recording our version of "Early My God, Without Delay," a retuned Isaac Watts hymn. You can almost hear the magic on the recording. It's far from perfect. In fact, it doesn't quite start on the right foot; the rhythms are a little stilted. But toward the end of the second verse, something happens. Rebecca Elliott sings, "Not life itself, with all her joys, will tempt my spirit move." Ambient guitars swell with a noisy growl and the thing comes together as she sings "My Maker and my helping Hand, all I need is You."

I remember my friend Paul, who coproduced the record with me, turning from the sound console to look at me as the last echoes of the plate reverb faded. We both knew it wasn't perfect, but we also knew something just happened.

It was the end of a week in that studio and near the end of a three-year-long process of rearranging and recording the hymns of Isaac Watts. We'd decided to record in analog, on an old Studer 2" tape machine, and we pretty much stuck to that plan. You hear warts and all since there was very little of the tuning and editing that's the standard fare of modern recording. It was, as Ani DiFranco once said, a record—as in a record of an event, the event being people in a room making music.

The White Arc was holy ground that week. Amid the music and the laughs were late-night talks about Jesus and resurrection. We talked life and marriage, the pain of chronic disease, the longing for children, the anxieties of parenthood, and the struggle of young artists to make ends meet. One of the singers' father passed away while we were there. We paused and prayed, making plans for her to come back to the studio when she was ready. She came back a few weeks later, singing, "My God has broke the serpent's teeth and death has lost its sting."

Flanagan's Ale House was a surprising sacred space. For those involved in weekly services it was our shared table almost every Sunday night. We'd watch the late game on big-screen TVs, or we'd sit on the patio and watch the crowd inside play furious trivia games. These dinners never had an agenda; we never asked each other accountability questions or had a discipleship plan. If we'd tried that, it wouldn't have worked; we had played four or five worship services by then and were exhausted. It was just the communion that happens between greasy burgers and buffalo chicken. A pub too was holy ground.

These musicians weren't just *my* community, of course. These were some of my wife's best friends too. Bonus aunts and uncles for my daughters. They were the friends who came to the hospital when our kids were born, who came and held them when we were exhausted. They sat in our living rooms for marriage mentoring. I officiated their weddings. We took vacations together and made life-changing decisions together. For me every milestone of life, career, and family intersected with music and particularly these musicians.

These were the mountain years of my life, where my sense of calling, community, and faith intersected with indescribable potency. When I left the ministry in 2015, I thought I'd stay connected to them. But things changed in ways that I couldn't anticipate and can't rightly describe now. Some of it was the natural gravity of life. Friends left to pursue their calling in New York or Japan, and ministries evolved under new leadership (as they should). But some of it can only be attributed to tragedy. Rounding the bend on midlife brings a whole different set of challenges and questions. For some of these friends, doubts arose because of lost faith. Discontent became moral failure. And while it was hard for me to name it at the time, I couldn't avoid the reality that some of that loss sprang from malice. Aspects of the disconnection that took place after 2015 were orchestrated for purposes of power and with the intent to wound. And wound it did.

The result is a profound sense of absence in my life. Like a heart transplant where someone forgot to put the new one in. It's the absence of a sacred space where friendship, creativity, and faith came together and provided a shared sense of meaning and belonging. The memories themselves have become something shaded and sad—nostalgic in the truest sense. It was Don Draper, on *Mad Men*, who described nostalgia as the pain from an old wound. The etymology is more like "homesickness." It's a burden of longing, a desire to go back to a place that no longer exists.

What's most maddening is the way loss introduces uncertainty and doubt in your mind. You look back at a devastated spiritual landscape on the other side of grief and wonder, *Was it ever real? Did it ever mean anything at all?*

———X———

The question God asks Elijah in the cave at Mount Sinai he asks all of us who find ourselves disillusioned and disoriented. "What are you doing here, Elijah?"

It's not unlike the question Jesus asks almost everyone he encounters in the Gospels, "What do you want?"

The answer isn't easily found. It's hard to say "I want to go back" because you know that the homeland you miss was built, to some degree, on illusions. Disillusionment, in this way, is a gift, albeit an unpleasant one. But naming something better is difficult too.

Elijah's answer is illuminating, not because he provides us with the right response (as if there were one) but because he shows a way forward: he complains. Loudly. Unapologetically. "I've given everything to you, God. But now I'm alone. I have no place to belong. No sacred spaces. Every memory is haunted. Everyone I loved and trusted has either turned on me or been crushed just like me."

I was raised not to complain, to see it as unvirtuous. I was also taught much about the holiness of God and what we were and weren't allowed to say or do before him. But there's a funny tension between my modern ideas and the attitudes of many of the fathers and mothers of our faith in the Hebrew Bible. They have an audacity, a willingness to argue, complain, or speak out of naked self-interest. Maybe that's one aspect of what it means to have a childlike faith: having the audacity to speak your mind in a relationship where the asymmetry of authority and control couldn't be starker.

God tells Elijah to walk out onto the mountain. It appears, from the text, that he doesn't, instead watching from within the cave as a violent wind kicks up enough to tear the mountain apart and shatter rocks. But God isn't in the wind. Then comes an earthquake, and still no God. Then comes fire, but again, God isn't in the fire (1 Kings 19:11-12).

In *The Message*, Eugene Peterson renders the refrain after each great sign appears, "God wasn't to be found in [it]." I've come to think this is the best way to understand the story—that the account of God's absence in the wind, quake, and fire is less about God and more about Elijah. He's a veteran of God's glory at Mount Carmel. He stands on what is maybe the holiest ground outside of Jerusalem, a mountain where God once before appeared spectacularly and renewed his covenant with Abraham's children. But Elijah can't see God in the spectacular anymore. The wind doesn't move him. The earthquake doesn't make him shiver. The fire leaves him cold.

As the final traces of wind quiet and the last of the flames turn to embers, a deep silence settles over the mountain. There, like a whisper, Elijah hears the voice of God. There's something different here, though, than the voice of God Elijah has been wrestling with up until now. He's aware of the divine presence in a new way and is at last drawn to it, walking to the mouth of the cave as if to get a better listen.

One reading of this story presents the contrast between the spectacle (wind, quakes, and fire) and silence as a test of the heart. It is, in this way, moralized. *Real* believers don't need the spectacles; they find God in quiet and silent ways. Some go so far as to apply it to the Christian life by using the spectacles as an emblem of the emotive mountaintop experiences described earlier in this book, contrasting them with the appropriate emblems of quiet—usually the sermons and books of the proponents of this view. Color me skeptical.

Instead, I read this story as descriptive of a journey of the heart. At Carmel the glory moved the prophet's heart and the hearts of

God's people. At Sinai, on the other side of suffering and loss, he was in a radically different place. It wasn't that he'd moved on from the spectacles, and the story isn't an indictment of having a heart moved by glory. Instead, it's a picture of the transformation that happens on the other side of grief. Perhaps it's not simply that God wasn't in the wind, (What would it mean that he was "in the wind" anyway?) Rather, it's that Elijah had lost the ability to find him in the wind. The spectacle had grown too complicated, too haunted with loss. Elijah's restless and grief-stricken heart needed silence on the other side of the storms of wind and fire to hear and recognize the voice of God.

Remarkably, the conversation they had before this transformation happens again, and it's echoed verbatim.

"What are you doing here, Elijah?" (v. 13).

"I've given everything to you, God. But now I'm alone. I have no place to belong. No sacred spaces. Every memory is haunted. Everyone I loved and trusted has either turned on me or been crushed just like me."

This time, though, there is one difference. Because Elijah has been struck again by the closeness of the divine presence, he's wrapped his head with his cloak. Like Moses on Sinai before him, he knows he can't look on the presence and live. This is my favorite moment of tension. God is near enough to strike a holy fear in Elijah, but this does not stop Elijah from remaining honest about his sorrow.

God's reply offers insight into life on the other side of loss and grief. "Go back the way you came," he begins (v. 15). This is, first of all, a subtle way of telling him, "Don't be afraid." Don't be afraid of abandonment, Jezebel, or death. It's also a call back to the place his journey began, which is to say a return to the faith that he loves (we'll pick this up in chap. 8). "Go back to the beginning," God says, "Return to where your journey began and go beyond that place to Damascus, where you'll find three young men who will take up the cause of redeeming Israel from its slavery to idols: Hazael and Jehu, new kings, and Elisha, the young prophet who will literally take up your mantle." Then he tells Elijah what may have been the greatest surprise and greatest promise of all: there are still seven thousand in Israel who have never bowed the knee to Baal (vv. 15-18). "Elijah," God says, "you're not alone."

The menace of Jezebel no longer looms over Elijah. The despair of loneliness has proven illusory. He does go back the way he came and devotes the rest of his life to these three young men.

Elijah came to Sinai despairing that his life and his dreams had come to an end. He left aware that the best parts of that dream— the hope of a renewed and restored Israel—were in God's hands and always had been. Seven thousand people Elijah had no idea existed remained faithful. The deeper awareness was that he needn't cling to the outcomes of whatever followed. The old cliché "God is in control" turns out to be true, but it may be something we only truly learn and that only liberates us after things fall apart.

Perhaps overshadowed by the heroics on Mount Carmel and the final spectacle of being taken to heaven in a chariot, we don't give enough attention to this moment in Elijah's life. Like disillusionment, despair is a disease only for true believers—dreamers and lovers. It hits when life falls apart, our sense of meaning and purpose fades when the people closest to us become incomprehensible or those we love disappear because of lies, brokenness, or death. Despair afflicts the lonely and forgotten, those whose prayers echo against a sky of concrete gray.

Those who've never known it themselves often encounter this deep darkness in others and are often mystified by it. The temptation to moralize it is powerful. "Put your hope in God," the cry of the psalmist, can quickly become, "Cheer up already," a sentiment likely to only deepen despair by intensifying a person's sense that something is wrong with them, their pain is invisible, and they are ultimately alone.

What we see at Sinai is both sobering and hopeful for both those who have suffered in spiritual darkness and those who love and want to support those suffering now. It simultaneously reveals that there is something solitary about that darkness and that like Elijah's journey first into the wilderness and ultimately to the cave on Sinai, the journey is taken alone.

Dante's *Inferno* has long been understood as the greatest literary expression of this kind of encounter with disillusionment and despair. The poet had been part of an aristocratic family in a time of great political turbulence in Italy. In 1285 he was pressured into marrying Gemma by a mixture of custom and political expediency. The woman he loved, known to history as Beatrice though her actual identity is uncertain, died suddenly in 1290. Political intrigue intensified in the next few years and Dante found himself on the wrong side of it in 1302, when he was sent into exile. Disillusioned by lost love, cast out by political enemies, and despairing, he began writing *The Divine Comedy*, of which *Inferno* is the first part. The opening canto describes the lostness of a derailed life.

> Midway upon the journey of our life
> I found myself within a forest dark,
> For the straightforward pathway had been lost.

I love the contemporary poet Mary Jo Bang's translation, which is starker and more arresting.

> Stopped in motion in the middle
> Of what we call our life, I looked up and saw no sky—
> Only a dense cage of leaf, tree, and twig. I was lost.

A few stanzas later, she translates:

> I don't know for certain how I entered it—
> I was so sleepy faced
> At the place where I took the wrong path.

No one chooses exile and no one chooses spiritual disillusionment. You simply awaken to find yourself there, wondering where the light has gone and where to turn next. In *Inferno*, Dante finds himself trapped between ravenous creatures and the gates of hell, discovering that the only way out of darkness is through it.

So it is with disillusionment. As much as we might run from it or distract ourselves, it lurks like the she-wolf and the leopard that hunted that great Italian poet. Our way out is into a place we fear, a journey that for Dante meant bearing witness to the great evils of the world on his way to redemption in paradise. For Elijah it meant finding solitude under the broom tree and on the fiery face of Mount Sinai. There he found out what we all can discover on the other side of grief—that he wasn't alone. That under the noise of storms and the heat of fires was the whisper of God, and that in the distance beyond us is always a remnant. We are never truly alone.

8

Homecoming at Galilee

A few hours before Jesus' arrest, shortly after the Last Supper, the disciples left the city.

Imagine a group of young men after a meal and a week like this. Warmed by the food, enlivened by the wine, their feet barely touching the ground as they talked about God's kingdom, the miracles and the confrontations of the past week, and the surreal lives they were living together. Did they notice Jesus was troubled? Did they know Gethsemane was to be his wilderness? His broom tree, only he really would experience God's departure?

He spoke to them on the way and said, "Tonight all of you will desert me" (Matthew 26:31 NLT). But how did Jesus say this? Did he wheel on them while they joked of war and of striking down the Romans? Did he cut one of them off mid-sentence while they were arguing about who was greatest in the kingdom? Or did he simply say it as they walked, letting the words gloss over most of them as they continued to laugh and talk?

We know that Peter heard Jesus and made his pledge that if all others abandoned him, he wouldn't. We've already been through what happened later that night, that when the rooster crowed, Peter was crushed by his frailty and failure.

But between the warning and the rebuke, Jesus said something else. "After I've been raised from the dead, I'll go ahead of you to Galilee, to meet you there" (v. 32).

Peter heard that too.

Capernaum sits on the north shore of Galilee. It may be the most charming place in all of the Holy Land. While it's often crowded, it has remained largely immune to the cheap tourism that can spring up around a religious pilgrimage.

Capernaum layers history atop history. Roman-era roads and walls and an ancient synagogue sit next to a beautiful, circular modern church that sits on stilts above the remnants of a Byzantine church that was in turn built on top of what are believed to be the remains of Peter's house. Each time I've come, the church has been busy with either a mass or the voices of a choir—often an impromptu performance from a traveling group. At the center of the church the floors are made of glass so pilgrims can see the excavation below.

The Sea of Galilee is beautiful. It's the lowest freshwater lake in the world, about six hundred feet below sea level, and remains an important commercial fishery today.

On one visit we came to Capernaum late in the day, near the time when the caretakers of the city were ushering people out and locking the gates. We took a short walk through the city and left, walking westward along the water and watching kiteboarders and windsurfers riding waves offshore. I found the steady hiss of the sea and the wind calming and centering after a day of noisy bus rides and busy tourist traps.

My friend Luke, who'd organized the trip with me, said, "Why don't we just take some time here." Everyone was tired and welcomed the idea of breathing the cool air coming off the water and sinking their toes into wet sand. My friend Sandra rolled her pants up and went wading out into the water. My wife and I sat on some rocks and let the waves wash over our feet.

The calm was broken by the loud "Woohoo!" from nearby. A massive rock jutted out over the water, and below was a deep pool where some surfers had been swimming and diving when we first arrived. This sound, though, came from my friend Dave. He was running across the black rock. He leaped off and hit the water with a splash, surfacing to wave and show he was all right before swimming out to another group of rocks. My friend Lachlan came sailing through the air after him.

It's hard for me to overstate how much I admire Dave. He's a poet, a person who feels deeply, and a fiercely loyal friend. I've often appreciated his freewheeling spirit that, far from making him flighty, seems to only deepen his connection to the present moment. We've joked for years that we pair up as friends a bit like Larry David and Jeff Garlin of *Curb Your Enthusiasm*, with me being the misanthropic Larry and him being the good-natured (if impulsive) Jeff.

When I remember the Sea of Galilee, I always think of him sailing through the air and into that water. "When will I get the chance to do this again?" he said afterward. "Get it while you can."

I often hear people tell those who are struggling or depressed, "You should get outside." There's some truth to it. Beautiful landscapes awaken something in us. There's something at once inviting and terrifying about being in a place with no walls to close in; every vista shows a valley where we could fall or be lost, and every shoreline shows depths that can suck us beneath and drown us forever. The sheer size of nature makes it hard to feel grandiose. But that's precisely what makes the outdoors liberating.

I've often found myself walking into conferences and boardrooms feeling enormous pressure to make myself feel and seem large. Everyone in the place—men and women alike—had a reason to make themselves into something larger than life, to take up space and project a self-image that said, *I'm competent; I belong here.* Those feelings evaporate in a storm or a dark wood. We feel rather small when we wade a few yards out in an ocean and feel the surge of the current or get hit with a tall wave. Even the greatest achievements of humanity versus nature—I think especially of Alex Honnold's remarkable climb up El Capitan in *Free Solo*—are remarkable precisely because of the asymmetry of an individual against nature.

And yet these encounters aren't dispiriting. Quite the opposite, when we stand on a mountaintop and feel the gravity of the landscape that sweeps out beyond us or when we dive into the ocean, the overwhelming feeling is of liberation and gratitude. These terrible and beautiful places could consume us; we are privileged to be alive and surrounded by them.

I don't think it's a coincidence that when God meets Elijah in his disillusionment, he sends him to Sinai, one of the most haunted and mystifying landscapes on earth. Likewise, it's no mistake that when Jesus told Peter what to expect after his resurrection, he sent him to Galilee.

The disciples were hiding in an upper room in Jerusalem, convinced that they too would be arrested because of their association with Jesus' "blasphemy" and the kingdom language that got him killed. On the morning of the third day, Mary Magdalene burst into the room in tears to announce that the tomb was empty. Jesus' body was gone.

Peter and John were out the door like a shot, John recounting decades later, not without some mischief, I think, that he got to the tomb first. The guards were gone and the stone rolled away. John believed Jesus had been raised, but uncertainty ruled the moment. Then Jesus appeared to Mary Magdalene, proving that he was indeed resurrected. She told the disciples, and later Jesus appeared to them as well. He showed them his wounds and breathed on them with the promise of the Holy Spirit.

These appearances were all strange, and you can tell that a certain amount of confusion and disorientation remained. They believed, but—at least in the book of John—it's not entirely clear they knew what came next. They were astonished, likely overwhelmed, and just . . . waiting.

One evening, maybe to get out some nervous energy, Peter said, "I'm going fishing" (John 21:3 NLT). The others joined, and they sailed out onto the Sea of Galilee. They fished all night but caught nothing, returning discouraged and weary. As they approached the shore, someone on the beach called out to them, asking, "Did you catch anything?" They said they hadn't, so he told them to cast their nets again. This time, the nets filled with fish so that Peter and the others couldn't haul them in.

Something clicked in John's mind. All of this has happened before.

Luke tells the other story in the fifth chapter of his Gospel. Jesus was in Galilee teaching, the crowds pressing in to the point of overwhelming him. Peter (then called Simon) had been fishing all night and was nearby washing his nets. His boat sat empty on the shoreline, and Jesus asked if he'd take him out a little way on the water so his voice would carry as he taught. Simon did as he was told. When Jesus was done teaching, he told him to go out further and cast his nets. Peter was tired. He'd fished all night and had just cleaned his nets; he'd have to repeat the whole exercise and as an experienced fisherman, he knew that the effort was pointless. Fishing had been fruitless the night before; it was the wrong time of day to be casting nets anyway. But he did as he was told and cast the nets again. The nets almost tore with the weight of the fish, and his partners had to come to help him bring in the catch.

Three years later John saw the mysterious figure on the shoreline and the overflowing nets after a hapless night. He turned to Peter and said, "It's the Lord" (John 21:7 NLT).

Peter dove right into the water and swam to shore.

I'll admit that this may well be overreading the text, but I can't help but obsess with one detail in this account: Peter leaping into the water.

Maybe it's a superfluous detail, maybe it shows Peter's impulsiveness once again. But when I read it, I can't help but think of yet a third moment between Jesus and Peter on the Sea of Galilee—one recounted in Matthew 14.

Jesus had performed the miracle of feeding the five thousand but had done so with grief in his heart. He'd just gotten word that his cousin, John the Baptist, had been beheaded. As Jesus dismissed the crowds, he sent the disciples ahead of him across the sea while he retreated into the mountains to pray. Late in the evening he watched their boat on the water, moving slowly because the waves and winds were against them. Jesus set out after them, walking across the waves.

The disciples were terrified when he came into view, certain that he was a ghost. Jesus calmed them down, assuring them it was him. Peter said, "If it's really you, tell me to come to you, walking on the water" (v. 28 NLT).

"Come," Jesus said.

Moments later, Peter stepped out of the boat, took a few steps, and then, seeing the waves and wind, grew afraid and began to sink. Jesus grabbed him by the hand. "You of little faith," he said. "Why did you doubt?" (v. 31). They walked to the boat and continued the journey across the Sea of Galilee.

The standard sermon on this passage goes something like this: Do you have the courage to step out of the boat? Peter did, but he sank when he took his eyes off Jesus and saw the waves. Can you keep your eyes on Jesus? Can you ignore the winds and waves of this life? If so, you too can walk on water! You can do great things for the Lord!

I'm not sure that's quite right.

There's a hazard in audacity. I believe Jesus knew Peter would sink and that the sinking was an essential part of Peter's story—and part of ours.

We spend an awful lot of time telling Christians to expect extraordinary things from their lives, and that's not entirely without reason. Jesus makes big promises about what faith can do and how we'll often receive what we ask for in faith. I'm just not sure that Peter walking on water is an example of that kind of faith.

Instead, it strikes me as an exercise in grandiosity followed quickly by a lesson in failure. Peter tells himself a story in which he is one of the heroes. He carries a sword, after all, and wouldn't hesitate to use it to defend his Lord. He belongs on top of the waves with Jesus. But notice that Jesus didn't ask him to get out of the boat; Peter asked him, and I think Jesus, knowing what would happen and maybe even a little amused by it, said, "Sure Peter, get out of the boat." Peter was audacious enough to dare great things, and he ran headlong into his frailty.

That's why I'm captivated by this moment on the Sea of Galilee in John 21. Whether intentional or not, I love the image of Peter diving into the water. He's still audacious, but he's not grandiose. He does not attempt to run across the water or make a leap of faith or stand proudly at the bow. He knows he is a mere swimmer. He dives into the water with the unrestrained joy of a child. He just wants to be with Jesus.

At the shore there's a speechless moment. Jesus invites them to eat a feast he prepared. The disciples were days into the anxiety and strangeness of Jesus' death and resurrection, tired from an empty night of fishing. And so, as to an exhausted Elijah under a broom tree, grace to the weary body came first.

After the meal, Jesus, Peter, and John took a walk. Jesus asked Peter a trifold question, confronting the obvious and awkward fact that Peter denied him on the night he was betrayed. "Do you love me?"

Like the questions "What do you want?" and "What are you doing here?" "Do you love me?" is fundamentally a question about desire, a way of asking "What do you love?" Each time, Peter answers, "Of course I love you," and Jesus replies with a variation of "Feed my sheep" (John 21:15-17).

After the third time, Jesus tells Peter, "The time is coming when you'll be bound and taken somewhere you don't want to go." If you love me, Peter, then my fate will one day be yours.

There were miracles in Peter's future, some so spectacular that they astonish almost as much as Jesus' own. But there would also be prison, beatings, and death. According to tradition, Peter demanded that the Romans crucify him upside down because he believed himself unworthy to die in the same manner as Jesus. In a sense it's one last instance of Peter highlighting the drama of a moment, though this time admirably. It's also the clearest sign that in the end Peter ultimately heard the story Jesus had been telling all along. Peter ended his life with no coronation, no parade, no throne; only inglorious participation in the death of his Teacher.

The cross means participation in future glory, for sure, but too often we gloss over the gritty reality of whips and nails. Hanging upside down, Peter would have not only suffered the normal suffocation that came with crucifixion, he'd have drowned in his own blood.

The fact that suffering is worth it—that we endure it for a promised future—should never be spoken glibly. That truth is costly, and it can lack credibility when it comes from those who haven't suffered deep loss yet. I'm not saying suffering isn't worth the glory that comes from participation in Jesus' death and resurrection. I'm saying we should never rush to that future fact without weighing the agonizing reality of present suffering, whether it's the physical punishment of persecution, the burdens of chronic disease or cancer, the sting of death, or the trauma of spiritual and physical abuse. Suffering carries people into deserts. It robs us of sleep. It creates gaps of incomprehensibility between us and those we love. Suffering leaves body and soul weary, restless, searching desperately for home.

Dante saw it rightly in his *Inferno*; the only way out of that suffering and darkness in this lifetime is to pass through it. The famous problem of pain is keeping the hope alive that you'll find God with you on the other side of that darkness even while going through hell. I know I have been in places where I couldn't keep hope alive myself. Sometimes a friend would have the right word at the right time to lift my spirits. Other times I just had to sit in the silence. In those times I can't say I'm sure how hope came back. It seemed out of my control. It may well have been.

However we make it through, the hope and prayer of going through suffering are that what we find on the other side of a shattered dream or an irreversible loss is a new resilience. Less ideological. Less certain. Less grandiose for sure. But assured, with feet on solid ground, that we had never been alone and never will be. Maybe the true gift of suffering is tuning our ears to hear God's whisper even when pain is shouting.

In early 2021 my father went into the hospital with strange symptoms that made us all think he'd had a stroke. For several weeks puzzled doctors failed to explain his difficulty keeping thoughts together or speaking. They found no signs of stroke. He went from hospital to occupational rehab to hospital—back and forth again and again. Finally, about three weeks in, a blood test showed some elevated enzymes. That was February 28, his seventy-fifth birthday. They decided to do a body scan to see if it might reveal the cause. The result was immediate. Cancer. Everywhere.

We were all shocked. Dad had seen doctors constantly. He'd had two knee surgeries in the past six months with no indications that anything like this was wrong. Somehow this had slipped by them, likely for a couple of years.

He died one week later. We were shell-shocked. I walked around in a daze for several weeks. I broke through the fog because of Jerry Seinfeld and a bottle of Barbicide.

I was getting my hair cut about a month after the memorial for my father. Motorhead was blasting over a stereo. Jesse, my hilarious barber, was telling stories about shark fishing from her San Diego days when the aura of the Barbicide—the neon-blue liquid barbers use to sterilize scissors and combs—caught my eye.

My mind immediately flashed to a scene from *Curb Your Enthusiasm*, the HBO comedy starring Larry David, the cocreator of *Seinfeld*.

Much of the plot of the show's seventh season is about Larry trying to reunite the cast of *Seinfeld* to tape a reunion episode for NBC. In one scene in episode eight, Larry is talking to Jerry after a table read of the reunion episode, apologizing for losing focus during the reading. Jason Alexander (George on *Seinfeld*) had been scratching his ear with a pen, and Larry was so disgusted he couldn't pay attention. Seinfeld shares Larry's, let's say, high standards of cleanliness. Jerry tells him, "You know, I like to keep my pens in a Barbicide. That blue liquid that the barbers have?" Obviously, it's an antiseptic, but the pair riff on why it's called "Barbicide." Larry quips that they kill themselves with it, and Jerry runs with it. "They can't take being a barber anymore, and they just down that blue liquid and that's it, they commit barbicide?"

Like much of *Curb*, this scene has the charm of two comedians trying to make each other laugh. The joke hit me at that moment as fresh as the first time I'd heard it, and I started laughing. Not a small laugh. It had an overwhelming, volcanic momentum. Jesse stepped back, unsure of what to make of the moment. That was when I realized tears were streaming down my face.

It was weird. I was blurring the lines between hysterical laughs and hysterical tears. Something I'd seen my kids do when they were small and tired, unable to manage their emotions. It dawned on me that I was the kid at that moment, crying for my dad.

I grew up in a house where much of our family life took place around the television. Our evenings had a consistent rhythm: *Night Court* and *Cheers* reruns from 7:00 to 8:00 and primetime TV after that. The primetime rotation changed, of course, as shows came and went. But for my high school years the two shows that couldn't be missed were *The X-Files* and *Seinfeld*. If we weren't home for some reason, the shows were taped on VHS or—later in high school—on the TiVo, which he somehow had years before anyone else.

Two decades later I could walk in the door of his house and still regularly find *Seinfeld* playing on the television. He'd quote episodes at dinner, send *Seinfeld* GIFs in text messages, or call me randomly to talk about a rerun he'd just watched.

Dad lived for comedy. For better or worse I was watching Mel Brooks, the Marx Brothers, and *Monty Python* from as early as I can remember. *Seinfeld* hit all the right comedy buttons for him—the Abbott and Costello dynamic of Jerry and George, the chimera of Harpo and Groucho embodied in Kramer, the pretzel-like plots and frenetic pacing. He never tired of it, and it was a love he passed on to all of us.

I saw that jar of Barbicide and remembered the joke from *Curb*, and as the laughing started I thought, *I should text him.* That was immediately followed by the weight of reality. He wasn't there.

The laughing stopped soon enough, and I managed to stifle the more embarrassing noises, wiping the tears and trying to pull myself together. I looked up to see Jesse, smiling awkwardly in the mirror, standing a foot or so back with the buzzing clippers still in her hand.

"You okay?" she asked.

I half-nodded. "My dad just died," I said. The words just kind of fell out of my mouth. "A few weeks ago," I said. "I just remembered this joke and . . ." I trailed off; there was too much to explain.

Jesse nodded. "Mine too. A few months ago." Then she added, "It always hits hard."

Nothing else needed to be said. For a silent moment it was as though we sat in ashes together, except instead of ashes, it was the clippings of my graying hair. We both drifted back into the here and now. AC/DC was now playing on the radio. The chatter at the other barbers' stations around us had gone on unabated. Jesse picked up her story about leopard sharks and got back to my hair.

It was a life-changing moment for me, though. For five years or more I'd sat in the chairs of therapists, counselors, and spiritual directors talking about the spiritual disorientation I'd experienced after leaving the ministry, and I'd heard the same thing over and over: "You need to learn to grieve."

I remember a moment about three years into that journey when I blurted out, "I don't know what the hell that means." I don't remember what the counselor said in response, but it didn't help. Looking back, though, I get it.

Those years after I left the ministry and started a nonprofit were hard for the church where I'd served. Sojourn, started as a home for misfits and ragamuffins, looked much like the churches we'd all left twenty years before. I wondered if a nineteen-year-old version of me would have made this his church home, and where the homeless young Christian malcontents were finding church today. Our lead pastor had resigned, but it tore the community apart. I wrestled with whether I should try to return to the staff to help lead it through the transition and find a new lead pastor, and while it didn't feel like the right call, still I dared to think I knew what that person—whoever they were—should do. In fact, if you'd pulled me aside at any point during those years, I would have talked your ear off about what the church ought to do to correct course.

In hindsight it feels as arrogant to me as it likely sounds to you. But what sits under the surface of that arrogance is the pain of a broken dream. It clung to my imagination like shackles.

Losing Dad disrupted my spiritual imagination. I experienced a finality unlike anything I'd ever encountered before. I saw him gasping for his last breaths. I watched his body covered with a sheet the morning he died. When I thought about texting him, the thought itself hit a brick wall; there was simply no way to reach him now.

That day in Jesse's barber chair opened the door to grief for me. Grief was not (as I often joked) the need to sit around and feel bad for a while. Rather, grief was an encounter with reality. Something was really and truly over. Even with the hope of resurrection my life on this earth will from here on be different; it will be without him, and no act of will or imagination can change that or make it easier.

It became clear in the weeks that followed that the same thing was true of my dream for Sojourn and had been so for a long time. This idea that we were always "one good conversation away" from fixing what was broken was a symptom of the disease that had infected the church. In reality we were never one conversation away because we were never having the same conversation. The people gathered around the tables never actually wanted the same things. It took an enormous amount of spiritual and psychological effort to pretend otherwise.

Sustaining cognitive dissonance takes enormous effort. You're constantly expending effort to tell yourself a story about why the stress is worth it, why things aren't so bad, why someone's intentions couldn't possibly be as malicious as they seem on the surface. Keeping the dream alive for yourself is hard enough. If you're also a leader, that exhaustion multiplies; you're not only carrying and managing your cognitive dissonance, you're also managing others', trying to hold a community together when malice or narcissism is distorting relationships and wreaking havoc. It is exhausting. That effort wanes slowly, but when it goes it's gone.

Grief means not only letting go of the dream but also letting go of the part of you that still thinks, *We could go back.* That the brick wall has a hidden door. The storyteller in you must die—the part that wants to imagine how things could be pieced back together. That you could at least somehow restore the feeling of what once was.

That longing is *nostalgia*: the pain from an old wound. The word itself means something like homesickness. In reality it's an illusion. A vision of what could be based on a story that never was true. If we nurture nostalgia, it can become the poison that keeps us from healing. From facing with strength the future that's coming anyway. Disillusionment is painful and can lead people to dark places, but at its healthiest it is a nostalgia killer.

Not long after that day in the barbershop, I was FaceTiming with my friend Reuben, a pastor I met in London years ago. I was feeling a strange mix of grief and relief—grief for the loss of both my father and my closest friends, relief for the way that sadness had become cathartic and freeing precisely once I stopped longing to rebuild. I talked about it with him, how disorienting it all was. "Am I crazy?" I asked.

"I don't know," he said. "I just have to tell myself that with every death in Christ, there's a resurrection."

I'd never heard anything truer.

When I stood on the shores of Galilee, my eyes were drawn constantly to the shoreline, to the smooth blue and gray stones at the edge of the water and the little piles of driftwood and dried leaves that the waves formed into thin, black arcs on the sand.

Though it was likely at Tiberius and not at Capernaum, I thought about a fire that burned on that shoreline and a meal served to tired and confused disciples. And I thought about that conversation between Peter and Jesus.

Jesus' questions were indeed a response to Peter's denials. They were also a kind of sacred confession about the past and future. Peter's dream died with Jesus' arrest at Gethsemane, and in asking Peter if he loved him the contrast to Peter was clear: Are you still with me, even with the dream broken? He was inviting Peter on a journey into the unknown and offering his death as the only certain thing in the years ahead. Was Peter willing to let go of the dream? Ready to journey into unknown lands?

I love the fact that *utopia* translates almost directly to "no place." It's like the failure of utopianism is baked right into the word itself.

All of our dreams are, in a sense, utopian. We dream of our own personal Mount Carmel or Mount Tabor, or maybe we dream backward, longingly and nostalgically for the places we've left behind. Peter's request of Jesus—Can we stay here?—is a utopian prayer. In the end no place can hold up to the demands of any dream because this side of the restoration of all things, we deal with entropy. Death creeps in and robs us of those we love. Sin and misunderstanding and fear and shame divide us. In time every place fails to become utopian because it's simply too real—too easily a home for ordinary human life and the consequences that accompany it.

When reality shatters the dream, there are two choices. One is an encounter with death. Elijah found his under a broom tree.

139

Peter found his at Gethsemane and Golgotha. The other is nostalgia—perverse homesickness that tries to keep the dream alive with promises of what might one day be restored.

I chose nostalgia for many years, imagining that what once was could be again. I paid the price for it too, with a sickness of the soul that brought me into a deep place of despair. The loss of my father was my encounter with death, and the grief that came afterward was the last gift my father ever gave me. It was the medicine that cured my nostalgia.

The promise of each of these stories—including mine—is that Jesus awaits us on the other side of grief. Peter found him on the shores of Galilee, right where he promised he'd be. Elijah found him in a whisper, not a maelstrom, while standing on the side of a mountain. His dream of restoring Israel was dead, but God had revealed a place for him in a larger story. Like Peter, there would be no coronation, no throne, no finality to the victories he'd win. And he'd only serve as a part of the story, not its climax. And yet somehow, like Peter being told he was marching to death or like Job facing an indignant God after questioning his judgment, Elijah seems to be happy to simply have that place—so long as he was being seen and known by God.

He had assurance that the story was being well-written when he came to Syria and met Elisha, the prophet who would carry on his ministry when he was gone. Centuries later he'd see what truly was the heart of that story on top of another mountain. On one side of him stood Moses, one of the fathers of his faith. On another stood Peter, James, and John, young men who'd spent their entire lives hearing and telling Elijah's story. Most gloriously he saw the shining face of Jesus.

It feels glib and maybe even indulgent to say that there is a deeper and richer experience of glory on the other side of grief. Maybe it's better to say that what's beautiful about life and faith shines brightest after we've seen what's dark about life and death. I worry that it's a cliché. And I struggle to believe it because of how often ideas like this were made transactional or worse, used as a cudgel to control others. Even so, I think there's something about grief, suffering, and disorientation that allows us to see and experience grace in ways we never could have before.

I want to think that on the other side of suffering, the church can find Jesus more beautiful, more glorious than they'd imagined or dreamed before. That the face of Jesus shines brighter when we see it on the other side of tears. That God, his angels, and the remnant of his people can sustain the weary and broken so they can make the journey from Golgotha to Galilee, from Mount Sinai to Mount Tabor. That there's glory on the other side of grief. That with every death in Christ there's a resurrection.

I want to believe; Lord, help my unbelief.

9

Land of My Sojourn

I'm Still Here

It's been two years since I had my emotional breakdown in a barber's chair. It's been almost eight years since I left my role at the church. Despite a thousand reasons for which things might be different, I'm still here. By that I mean I'm still a part of Sojourn Church in Louisville, but I mean a lot more than that too.

It's not simple to account for why that's the case, though. The process of writing this book has helped me reckon with it.

This isn't, in fact, the book I set out to write. I thought I was writing a book about the Sermon on the Mount and the ways that vision of the Christian life feels more essential than ever in a post-Trumpian, secularized world. That vision is no small part of the reason why I'm still here, and the up-and-down road of faith in

142

the last seven or eight years has helped me make sense of its message in new ways.

Whatever we might make of the church in all its brokenness or of evangelicalism and its addiction to celebrity and hype, the Sermon on the Mount's moral, spiritual, and ethical vision remains incredibly compelling as a vision of the heart, mind, and life of Christ. From its very beginning it offers an account of life with God that embraces the tragic. "Blessed are the poor in spirit, for theirs is the kingdom of heaven." My friend Jonathan Pennington has beautifully argued that what is often translated as "blessed" is better understood as "flourishing"—that in each beatitude we're given a description of the human condition that is counterintuitively a place in which we can experience wholeness and fullness through life with God.

Jesus goes on to dismantle the way we think about ethics and judging others, he calls out reactionary faith that lives with a spirit of scarcity or anxiety, and he invites us into a spirituality that is quiet, resists performative action, and cultivates intimacy with him. It's beautiful counterprogramming to contemporary spirituality, which is probably a good reminder that contemporary spirituality isn't anything new.

The Sermon on the Mount was an anchor for me not because of my great faith in it but because of its magnetic hold on my imagination. I don't know if I'll ever get around to writing that book (I hope I do), but in any case it's a big reason I'm still here.

I'm also still here because of friendship. The subject came up on New Year's Eve this year when I was sitting with friends at a small

party. Someone asked a dangerous question for our group, which
was made up mostly of people who've had their own personal and
spiritual lives disrupted by the turmoil at our church in the last
few years: "How does your life look different than you imagined
it would a decade ago?"

I thought back to 2012 and began to run down the list of names
of those I'd spent most of my waking hours with both inside and
outside work. Each name had a sad story attached to it. They may
have quit during the conflict, been forced to resign and move out
of town; some were fired for moral failure; others left because of
staff dysfunction. One was gone because of the divisive power of
politics and online conspiracy theories. I finished my list and sat
silent for a moment, looking at my friends' stunned eyes.

"But I'm glad I'm here," I said. They laughed, "We are too," one said.

I think about the sustained and restored friendships with an
enormous amount of gratitude. None of them were healed as a
matter of course, and some of them took a great deal of risk and
vulnerability on both of our parts.

One moment in particular seemed like an important hinge for the
restoration of our friendships. It was on the day that Sarah and I
found out that another friend in ministry had just been fired for
moral failure. This was someone we'd loved and invested a lot of time
in, and it broke our hearts for his family and the church that was
affected. We had very little to offer one another in terms of comfort
or cheer that night, and Sarah insisted we call two of our friends.

We hadn't spoken to either of them for a long time. They lived
nearby and were leaders in the church who we'd trusted as people

who could show up, care, and listen when people were hurting. But they'd also been on the other side of a divide among our friends after the resignation of our pastor. We took the risk to call them, and they took the risk to show up and listen to us as we wept. The conversation about that day's events turned into a much broader conversation about our broken hearts, our loneliness, and our shattered faith. They offered no prescriptions. Mostly, they listened and said, "Me too."

It was an experience that woke me out of a kind of selfishness that had descended along with the loneliness and despair; I hadn't taken much time to think about the impact of all of the church's turmoil on others. The more we talked, the more we found common ground in our sense of disorientation, loneliness, and spiritual confusion.

That friendship became deeper and stronger, and it was a bridge toward other restorations in the months and years that followed. He was one of the people sitting in the room on New Year's Eve when I recounted the list of all those folks who were gone.

But there are many other friendships that endured or were restored. I still count Nathan, the original leader of our prayer group and the guy who came up with the name Sojourn, among my closest friends, and I would count most of the dozen or so original members of that group as friends as well. There are plenty of relationships I'd love to see restored, and even in the most serious cases where the division runs deep, I hold on to some hope for restoration.

My friend Makoto Fujimura, a painter and writer, has often talked about the Japanese art of *kintsugi* as a metaphor for the work of grace. In the art form a broken ceramic vessel—a cup, jar, or vase—is mended with gold. The finished product still shows the scars from the break, but the scars are filled with streaks of gold. A finished *kintsugi* vessel is more beautiful and valuable than the original.

These restored friendships feel like *kintsugi* artifacts. Sin, uncertainty, misunderstanding, and sorrow caused rifts and disconnections. The grace that healed them made them much more beautiful.

I'm also still here because, in the years since 2016, I've had good pastors.

I left the staff of Sojourn in 2015 expecting to continue to worship at the campus where I'd served for fifteen years. But we thought, for the sake of a healthy transition, we'd attend a different campus—Sojourn East—for a few months. For a variety of reasons those few months became permanent, and after Sojourn's lead pastor's resignation in 2017, all of the Sojourn campuses became independent churches. We've been at Sojourn East ever since.

Like most Christians who were once in ministry, I show up on Sunday mornings with a chorus of opinions in my head about how things are done and what's said and what's sung. These days they sound an awful lot like Statler and Waldorf, from *The Muppet Show*, full of opinions that no one needs. I do my best not to listen to them or let them out.

I'm committed here not because it remains just like the church we planted twenty years ago. It's very different, and I'm fine with that. And not because it reaches and serves those displaced

Christians I was worried about twenty years ago either. In a way, it does—we've just all gotten older, had kids, and are living in different neighborhoods. But it's also decidedly more in the cultural mainstream. I'm fine with that too.

I'm committed here because this remains the place where we belong—not because of the cultural trappings but because of the people who have been the anchor points of our life and faith. That includes these friends, and it includes our pastors.

In the most turbulent moments of the post-2016 years, the pastors at Sojourn East showed up to care for us. They prayed for us, they helped me not only understand that it was okay to feel anger and doubt but also to feel safe as an angry and doubting person. They showed up on doorsteps and living rooms in critical moments. They were patient and persistent. They knew times when despair was setting in, and they remained firmly committed to walking with us through it.

One of the stark realities of the experience of disorientation is that not everyone gets through it. I know many people whose status as true believers was disrupted by pain and suffering and whose faith never recovered. As someone who stood in the darkness, that makes sense to me. Others hit that point of despair and lose hope altogether, and sadly that makes sense to me too.

In May 2020 I got a phone call that I'll never forget. It was my friend Cliff, a former Sojourn pastor, calling to tell me that our friend Darrin Patrick was dead.

Darrin was the planting pastor of The Journey in Saint Louis, a former vice president of the Acts 29 church-planting network, and an influential writer and speaker. Darrin conflicted with his elders and leaders for many years, and a final-straw incident tipped the scales, giving the elders the catalyst to remove him from leadership in 2016 and begin a process of repentance and restoration.

I'd known Darrin since 2004, and we'd been friends from the beginning. I used to joke that I liked being his friend *and* was glad I didn't work for him, a joke Darrin always got (though he didn't always laugh) because he had some degree of awareness about his flaws.

We lost touch long before his removal from leadership—probably in 2012 or so—but out of the blue in 2017 he called me. I figured he was calling to ask what was happening at Sojourn since we were in the middle of our tumultuous season, but he didn't. He asked about me, how my transition out of ministry was going, and what was in my head. I was honest with him about the disorientation I was feeling at the time. When I asked how he was, he blurted out his story—the long-term conflicts, the lapses in judgment, the sense of failure and humiliation.

He asked me if I had it all to start over again, would I still want to plant the church? I didn't have an answer and neither did he.

We made an odd couple of friends—me, the burned-out former member of a toxic culture, and Darrin, the fallen leader of a toxic culture. But in a season of life where I had few friends who could understand what was happening, Darrin certainly could. I remain puzzled by our friendship even now. Again, I have no illusions about what it was like for some members of his former staff, and yet in a season of loneliness and isolation he showed up as a friend.

It's a good example of the complexity of human nature; none of us are just one thing, pure villain, pure hero.

Not long after reconnecting, Darrin began working with another pastor on launching a ministry for pastors that was aimed at helping them prevent or recover from burnout. I spent much of 2018 and 2019 collaborating with him, developing online content, and producing interviews. We traveled back and forth to Charleston together every few months to develop the project.

My last trip to Charleston with him was in December 2019. We went to dinner at a tourist trap on Sullivan's Island and walked out on the sand afterward. Like most of our conversations, we were talking about the unexpected midlife crossroads we were facing. He wasn't sure if he was in the right place. I wasn't sure how I'd do what I was doing forever either. Darrin got teary-eyed and said, "I know I've burned a lot of bridges and hurt a lot of people. I know you've been through some things too. You didn't have to be my friend during all this but you did." He thanked me for being his friend, and I did the same. It felt like a holy moment, and still does.

Our next time together was supposed to have been at the end of March, but Covid-19 canceled the trip. We continued some production work from a distance, looking to pick things back up again by summer. We talked on Monday, May 5, about rebooking the trip in June, picking things up with masks and Lysol and lots of hand sanitizer. Then Cliff called two days later, telling me Darrin was gone.

I won't speculate as to what was happening in Darrin's head or heart that day. I know his story well—the wounds he'd been addressing in his own life; the ways he'd hurt others; the pressure, pride, and shame that come with being a leader and a leader who "fell." But none of that tells me or you what story he was telling himself. All I can say with any confidence is how losing him affected me. Because it hit me like an earthquake.

The Covid-19 lockdown had silenced much of the normal noise of my world—the travel for work, the constant movement, the steady flow of interactions with people and information. It had all been still for nearly two months, but somehow this added stillness, this sudden absence of a friend, shook me to my core. In that absence I could hear and feel the deep discontent within me, my own unfinished and unresolved stories, and the many ways I was ignoring or drowning out the sound of my own tired, sad voice.

I don't pretend to know what pushed Darrin to the brink. All I know for sure is that when I lost my friend, I encountered my own fragility, and—to borrow another phrase from Rich Mullins— even in my weakness, I was not as strong as I'd thought.

I broke, and yet I never shattered. The cracks opened up in my heart and life, but the people I loved—many who couldn't have imagined what was taking place internally—showed up to keep me from completely falling apart. They helped me find my broom tree; they fed me bread and water and told me to sleep. They are the reason I'm still here—both here on this earth and here as a member of Sojourn East, a church that grew out of the one I planted twenty-three years ago.

It's not a perfect church. I'm sure you could find people who could write their own frustrated and disorienting accounts of faith from within our community. But it's been the source of grace for us.

I'll never forget a conversation to that effect from last fall. A few of us had just heard from a family who was returning to our church after a season elsewhere, during which they'd experienced serious spiritual and emotional abuse from church leaders. As we processed their story, someone said, "Sojourn East . . . not so bad after all." We all laughed. Someone suggested making it the church's official slogan. I doubt they'll print it on any T-shirts, but it's good enough for me. It's the kind of church I want to be a part of. No grandiose promises. I want deep faith and deep conviction, but I also want room for tired people who sometimes struggle to catch their breath before they make the walk from the parking lot to the pew. If one or two of the pastors are on that journey too, all the better. I want to know what Henri Nouwen called "wounded healers" because they sound like the kind of folks I can trust.

I also think, in a weird way, I'm still here because of the disillusionment itself. There's something about the experience that provides a kind of hidden gift. On the other side of it, one doesn't lose their sense of gratitude for what is good and beautiful—friendships, experiences, that sort of thing—but you do hold them much more loosely. It's as though disorientation and restoration result in a future-oriented sense of pleasure in the present. Yes, this experience of this moment is good. But it may not be good tomorrow, and that's okay because it doesn't have to be. Your time horizon gets longer. I don't need perfection so long as I have hope.

We simultaneously feel grateful for a good thing, sorrowful for that sad world in which the good emerges, and hopeful for something better and more beautiful in the age to come. I don't feel or remember all that perfectly or all at once. But it is there.

Bill Mallonee's song "Resplendent" has captured that for me better than anything else I've encountered. It's a narrative about someone living in the Dust Bowl trying to survive its harshest elements. It's taken away his son and his wife. He then asks,

> How much of this was meant to be?
> How much of the work of the devil?
> How far can one man's eyes really see
> in these days of toil and trouble?

These are the questions of all who suffer as people of faith. Then, toward the end he offers what I think is maybe the most honest, sober description of the Christian life. On the other side of grief he writes,

> I can make you promises
> if you don't expect too much
> Yes, and I will run the distance
> if you'll please, please excuse my crutch.

I find myself praying those words often. Because whatever else this journey means for me, like Elijah and Peter, God is not done with my story. Elijah was not left to meditate in the presence of God on Mount Sinai for the rest of his life. Peter doesn't recline on the shores of Galilee and enjoy spiritual enlightenment. Instead, they're sent back into a dangerous world where suffering will come and they will continue to encounter darkness.

By God's grace. I hope to do the same.

I was sharing the ideas in this book with a friend recently, and he pointed out that it shares common themes with Christian literature about first- and second-stage spirituality—the idea that most people emerge from a period of suffering or failure to approach the second half of their life in a new way. I laughed and said, "Yeah, maybe, but if so, it's just the first half of that book." I don't have much guidance for the second half yet. Hopefully, I get to learn that part next. I look forward to it, and I don't take that for granted anymore either.

I still find my story incredibly mysterious and confusing at times. Like Bill, I wonder how much of it was orchestrated by God to shape me and those I love in a certain direction. And how much of it was simply the work of the devil. I don't think there's a simple answer to that question, and if God has one, he sure hasn't been forthcoming about it.

But I have the faith to believe that while the God of grace doesn't always heal every wound, he certainly will excuse every crutch. And so I'm still here, making this journey. Through the land of my sojourn.

Acknowledgments

This book is about forty thousand words. It probably took writing two hundred thousand words to get this draft. Writing this book was a wild ride not only for me but also for the friends and loved ones who put up with the neurotic process it required.

Thanks most of all to Sarah, for reading the early drafts, telling me when they weren't ready, and encouraging me to keep writing. Thanks to Dorothy and Maggie for being such joy and light in dark years.

Thanks especially to Michael Morgan for his editing help. I couldn't have brought the project home without him. Thanks to Don Gates, who's always been my most faithful advocate and friend as a writer. Thanks as well to Ethan McCarthy and Cindy Bunch at InterVarsity Press for your faith, encouragement, and your long-suffering.

Thanks to Kevin Jamison for being my pastor.

Thanks to Nathan Quillo for inviting us all into your living room, beginning our sojourn.

Thanks to Lachlan Coffey, Ben Mast, Scott Slucher, and Kyle and Hilary Noltemeyer for your friendship.

Thanks to Jonathan Pennington for your help on the book I ended up not writing.

Thanks also to Brad House, Bob Stewart, Mike Frazier, David Zahl, Reuben Hunter, and Rich Plass.

Thanks to my friends and coworkers at *Christianity Today*, especially Erik Petrik, Tim Dalrymple, Russell Moore, and Joy Beth Smith.

Also by the Author

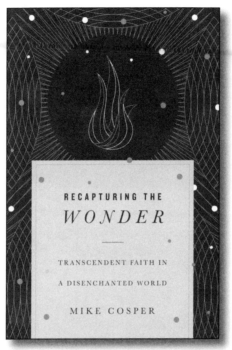

Recapturing the Wonder
978-0-8308-4506-4